HUNGARY

IN TRANSFORMATION TO
FREEDOM AND PROSPERITY

BLUE RIBBON COMMISSION

Project Hungary

HUNGARY

IN TRANSFORMATION TO
FREEDOM AND PROSPERITY

Economic Program
Proposals of the Joint
Hungarian-International
Blue Ribbon Commission

April 1990

Hudson Institute

Published under the auspices of the
Blue Ribbon Foundation, Budapest

Published by
Hudson Institute
Herman Kahn Center
P. O. Box 26-919
Indianapolis, Indiana 46226

ISBN   1-55813-035-7

Printed in the United States of America

Members of the Blue Ribbon Commission

Márton Tardos (Co-Chair). Economist, Institute of Economics of the Hungarian Academy of Sciences; President, Financial Research Ltd.; *Hungary.*

Sylvia Ostry (Co-Chair). Economist; Chairman, Center for International Studies, University of Toronto; former Chairperson, Economic Council of Canada; former Ambassador to Multilateral Trade Negotiations; former Head of Economics and Statistics of the OECD; *Canada.*

Iván T. Berend. Economic historian; President, Hungarian Academy of Sciences; *Hungary.*

Enikö Bollobás. Associate Professor of Literature and American Studies, University of Szeged; expert on the economic and social roles of women; *Hungary.*

Csaba Csáki. Agricultural economist; Rector, Budapest University of Economic Sciences; *Hungary.*

Guillermo de la Dehesa. Economist and lawyer; C.E.O., Banco Pastor; Chairman of Gas Madrid; Vice-Chairman of Goldman Sachs Europe Ltd.; Member of the Group of Thirty and Governor of the Centre for Economic Policy Research, London; former Spanish Secretary General of Commerce and Secretary of Finance; expert on privatization; *Spain.*

Pierre S. du Pont IV. Lawyer; former U.S. Congressman, Governor of Delaware; boardmember of Hudson Institute; candidate for the Republican Party nomination for President (in 1988), *United States.*

Herbert Giersch. Economist; former President of the Institute for World Economy of the University of Kiel and professor of economics at the University of the Saarland; member of the Academic Advisory Council to the West German Ministry of Economic Affairs; *Federal Republic of Germany.*

Janos Peter Hrabovsky. Agricultural economist; former Senior Policy and Planning Coordinator of the Food and Agricultural Organization of the UN; *Australia.*

Géza Jeszenszky. Historian and political scientist; Professor of International Relations and Dean of Social and Political Studies, University of Economics; *Hungary.*

Koichi Minaguchi. President, Nomura Research Institute, Inc. and the Tokyo Club Foundation for Global Studies; *Japan.*

István Orbán. Pharmaceutical company executive; Manager and C.E.O., Egis Pharmaceutical Corporation, a state-owned enterprise in Budapest; *Hungary.*

György von O'sváth. Economist and lawyer; Head of Division, Commission of the European Communities; Co-chairman, EC Research and Documentation Center, Budapest; *Federal Republic of Germany.*

Sung Sang Park. President, Korea Institute of Economics and Technology; *Republic of Korea.*

László Rózsahegyi. Engineer and inventor; Founder and C.E.O, ROLITRON, one of Hungary's largest and most successful private enterprises; *Hungary.*

Hans Seidel. Financial economist; Director, Institute for Advanced Study, and Professor, University of Vienna; *Austria.*

George Soros. Financier and philanthropist; President, the Soros Fund Management, New York; *United States.*

György Surányi. Economist; Deputy President, Planning Office; *Hungary.*

István Szalkai. Financial economist; Professor, Banker Training Academy, Budapest; former Vice President of the National Bank of Hungary; *Hungary.*

Sir Alan A. Walters. Economist; Director, Putnam, Hayes and Barlett, Inc., Washington D.C.; Professor of Economics, John Hopkins University; columnist for the *London Times*; ex-chief economic advisor to Prime Minister of UK, 1980-84 and 1989; *United Kingdom.*

Contents

Blue Ribbon Commission Meetings

Indianapolis (top) Participants convene for a plenary session during meetings in January 1990 at Hudson Institute. (above) Meetings in Indianapolis were held at the Herman Kahn Center, headquarters of Hudson Institute. (right) An informal meeting between sessions outside one of the working groups. At center is Dr. Márton Tardos, BRC co-chairman.

Indianapolis (right) Commission members Enikö Bollobás, Pete du Pont, and Janos Hrabovsky participate in discussion. (below) BRC Co-chairs Márton Tardos and Sylvia Ostry--at right in picture--preside over a plenary session. To their right are Hudson Senior Fellow Bruce Chapman, Sir Alan Walters of the BRC, and Richard Judy, Director of Hudson's Center for Soviet and Central European Studies. (bottom left) Elemér Hankiss and Paul Demeny direct a meeting of Working Group 5 on social policy. (bottom right) Commission co-director Paul Marer addresses a dinner gathering.

Brussels *(above, left, and below)*
The Blue Ribbon Commission
reconvened in February at the
headquarters of the European
Community in Brussels.

Budapest *(top) BRC member Pete du Pont--at center in picture--confers with Hudson's Bruce Chapman. To du Pont's left is László Rózsahegyi of the BRC. (above) A BRC meeting in Budapest. At the head table are Paul Marer and Co-chairs Sylvia Ostry and Márton Tardos. (right) Hudson's Richard Judy, Tardos, and Richard Rahn of the U.S. Chamber of Commerce talk between sessions in Budapest.*

Foreword

Formation of the Commission

1   In the summer of 1989 several Hungarians and expatriates conceived the idea of a "blue ribbon commission" to help a new democratic government to chart the heretofore unexplored route from a centrally directed economy, which had proven a dead end, to a market economy, where most Hungarians clearly desire to arrive. The enthusiasm for such a project subsequently was caught by several domestic and international research institutions. In the autumn of 1989, these institutions jointly agreed to convene this particular Blue Ribbon Commission (the "BRC"), whose analytical report and "Action Program" follow.

2   A "blue ribbon," in certain Western usage, connotes a "first place prize" or "best performance" standard; a blue ribbon commission, therefore, is a panel of academic experts and individuals of other distinctive achievements in a given field. Such a panel was assembled to address the means for effecting the economic recovery and transformation of Hungary, and for doing so with a minimum of pain during the transition.

3   Those asked to serve on the Commission were eager to accept. They have served without pay, and some have also paid their own expenses or helped raise private philanthropic corporate funding to support the Commission. This is also true of some of the other experts and advisers brought together to participate in the BRC process.

4   The panel, though initiated by sponsoring institutions (see Appendix A and B for acknowledgments), is independent and beholden to no one for its mandate or deliberations. The Hungarian and

international participants from various universities, public policy institutes, governments, businesses, financial institutions, and international organizations were invited to join the project as individuals and not as spokespersons for any organization with which they might be affiliated.

Unusual Features of This Project

The reliance on volunteers and private philanthropy in this project   5
not only expresses the confidence of the Blue Ribbon Commission participants in the ultimate outcome of the historic changes ahead in Hungary but is also an example of how the private voluntary sector of societies worldwide can assist in meeting public needs in ways that government often cannot.

There are several other unusual, and perhaps even unique, fea-   6
tures of the BRC. Within Hungary, its very convening showed a new patriotic determination to meet the economic challenge with goodwill and common purpose. This spirit cut across the political spectrum, even though the latter stages of the BRC's deliberations took place in the midst of the first free Hungarian election campaign in over 40 years.

While some debates in the BRC were among Hungarians, others   7
were among the international participants and often the "alliances" changed from issue to issue. But the sense of overall unity among the participants of all persuasions and backgrounds prevailed. Although there were some subjects on which complete accord could not be reached, the Action Program overall exhibits a clear, coherent thrust. That this degree of agreement could be reached by such a divergent group should send a message of hope to Hungarian citizens and to the world.

The sustained participation on the Commission of sympathetic   8
foreign friends of Hungary is another unique feature of the BRC. Many are simply advocates of liberty and a market economy; others are expatriates with a similar philosophy. All look to Hungary to set an example for other countries that are undergoing

an economic transformation or may do so soon. These international BRC members and advisers were asked to describe the experiences of economic development in their countries and to draw common lessons.

9   The BRC Action Program is also unique in its ambition to pull together in one place so many of the interactive elements of a national economic transition. This ambition springs from recognition that success in any one economic sphere can be undermined by failures in other spheres unless the program as a whole is coordinated as to philosophy, content, and timing.

Uses of the Action Program

10   The BRC Action Program is intended to reach:

- the new government of Hungary to be formed shortly after the democratic elections that were held in March and April, 1990;

- individuals, organizations, and parties in Hungary that are interested in obtaining an independent view on Hungary's current economic and social situation and policy options; and

- individuals and organizations outside Hungary that have intellectual, business, or policy interests in the transformation of communist societies generally and of Hungary in particular.

11   It is up to the newly elected representatives of the Hungarian people to decide whether to use any or all of the Blue Ribbon Commission's study as they prepare the economy for its historic transformation. We on the Commission, in any event, have been honored to be associated with this inspiring challenge.

Chapter 1

LEGACIES, OBJECTIVES, PRINCIPLES AND THE POLITICAL FRAMEWORK

Crisis in the Inherited Economy

12   The centrally planned economy of Hungary has failed. Forty years of political and economic dictation have left the present generation with a monumental economic crisis--and the challenge to meet it with totally new policies. The pervasive economic role of the state, the discouragement of private initiative, and a legacy of coercive economic relations with other Eastern countries have left the economy in a perpetually weak and dependent condition, totally at odds with Hungary's promising potential.

13   The present historic moment of restored freedom in politics offers the opportunity and necessity of a clean break with the past in economics as well. This report is designed to provide a possible guide to a strong and sustainable economic revival, commensurate with the desires and capabilities of the Hungarian people.

14   The first requirement is for the public and its new leadership to understand the seriousness of the crisis. The second requirement is to summon the patience and resolve to undergo, as rapidly as practical, a methodical transformation of economic life. Only this will allow new growth and achieve lasting stability.

15   Roots of the present disorder are found in the communist political and economic system imposed upon Hungary. In the first two

decades of the regime, rapid but unbalanced economic growth was achieved through ambitious capital investment plans, ideologically dictated nationalization of the private sector, and a 19th century industrialization strategy. This economic model was soon exhausted.

Since 1968 and the "New Economic Mechanism," which only   **16** partially decentralized economic decision-making, Hungary has seen repeated well-intentioned half-measures of reform of the exhausted command model. Politics did not permit full transformation. But an economy only partially free, like a people only partially free in their political life, ultimately is demoralized when false hopes are dashed by experience.

Today, Hungary has a structure of production which does not   **17** match demand on the world market or even at home. The inflation rate is in the double digits. The currency is not convertible. Goods and services are not competitive abroad. Real wages have fallen, and with them the average person's standard of living. Hungarians are burdened with a $20 billion foreign debt, $2000 per capita, one of the highest in the world.

The economy that has produced these results is still characterized   **18** by dominance of state decision-making and lack of significant market motivation. Production is greatly influenced by state regulation, including direct and indirect controls on prices, limitation on resource use, and state trading obligations with the countries of the Council for Mutual Economic Assistance (CMEA).

Output is overwhelmingly dominated by state enterprises. The   **19** proportion of gross domestic product (GDP) channeled through public coffers is 60%, a share related to redistribution in the form of transfers and subsidies to and from enterprises and consumers. While the proportion of those employed in industry is similar to those in the advanced market economies, the structure of industrial production is outmoded. Hungary manufactures goods that often cannot be sold on the world market, or, if sold at all, are sold only at deep discounts in price. International trade, though notably amounting to a large share of GNP, has not been sufficiently competitive to realize gains comparable to those enjoyed by countries with market economies. Bartering within the CMEA certainly has contributed to this international trade deficiency. Agriculture represents a relatively high proportion of employment in the population--some 10-12%. Employment in services, on the other hand, is relatively low.

20   In this economy, whole sectors of society that in a market economy contribute to economic health, such as a vibrant entrepreneurial sector, have been unable to struggle to their feet. New technologies, which in the West liberate forces of productivity and add to national wealth, here have been thwarted by a system of control that is hostile to innovation. Qualitative growth therefore has languished. An untold number of new, high quality jobs have never been created in Hungary due to the failure to modernize economic operations and to encourage new private businesses.

The Opportunity and the Challenge

21   Most of this report deals with the technical changes needed to transform Hungary's failed economy to a successful market system. But the moral basis of a free economy, like the moral basis of democratic pluralism, must not be forgotten. Just as the political institutions of democracy will survive only as individuals take personal responsibility for their citizenship, so, too, will the free economy succeed only as the individual contributes his own self-discipline and initiative, enabling himself personally to take advantage of the new opportunities of freedom, and through his efforts, also facilitating the success of others.

22   A centrally planned economy reproaches certain useful human ambitions and punishes practical virtues. Economic competition, which puts high value on the satisfaction of customers and thereby helps lead to qualitative improvements in products and services, is discouraged. Personal economic initiative and the aspiration to use one's abilities to better one's own life, and that of one's family, are suppressed. On the other hand, seemingly attractive public aims, such as government assurance of job security and govern-

ment prevention of trade abuses, turn out to stifle personal responsibility, cover up for waste and stimulate bureaucratic indif-
ference.

Government cannot fulfill people's lives. What a wise govern-   23
mental system can do is to create the trustworthy, confidence-
inspiring institutions that permit individuals to fulfill their own
lives. While restructuring the existing economy is important, of
even greater significance is the task of unleashing the power of
Hungary's heretofore frustrated potential and building a dynamic
entrepreneurial economy.

In Hungary that will not be easy. But it is possible if right decisions   24
are made in the coming months and years. The welcome elections
of 1990 return political institutions in Hungary to the people by
providing once again for competition. The mandate of the new
government is to support this process of democratization by
erecting alongside it a market economy. In a free society, these
institutions reinforce one another and add depth to social and
personal life.

Hungary is not alone in its economic ordeal, nor is it alone in its   25
hopes for a better future. It should not count on large foreign
governmental assistance nor assume that even necessary assistance will be granted if correct decisions are prevented or post-
poned by the new government. Sacrifices, unfortunately, will be
necessary.

However, we believe in a bright economic future for Hungary and   26
consider that wise policies to encourage the virtues of a free
market will be its sturdiest foundation. These hopes for Hungary,
indeed, are linked to the aspirations of others in the developing
European polity and the integrated world economy. In reaching
this future on such a basis we call upon the whole international
community to help Hungary in making the difficult adjustment
that lies ahead.

Main Objectives and Principles of the New System

27   The transformation of Hungary's political system and the trans-
      formation of the economic system are mutually dependent and
      reinforce one another. A precondition for Hungary's recovery is
      political leadership to effect the transformation of the economic
      system. Prolonging the economic crisis would impede the process
      of democratization, political stabilization, and effective govern-
      ance.

28   In essence economic transformation requires that the dominant
      role of the state, with its myriad of arbitrary and often incompat-
      ible priorities, be replaced with a system in which economic
      decisions are primarily made by individuals and enterprises,
      coordinated by a self-regulated market mechanism and consumer
      choice. At the same time, the transformation cannot be accom-
      plished without restoring to the state some of the powers which
      had been dissipated in the course of the reform. Transform-
      ing and stabilizing the economy requires a strong government.

29   Although the full transformation will take time, a market economy
      should be created with all deliberate speed for the following
      reasons:

      • The values of political pluralism are most in harmony
        with autonomous, decentralized economic decision making.

      • A market economy promotes such values as entrepre-
        neurship, tolerance, and a willingness to compromise.

      • The experiences of the developed countries show that
        market economies, guided by appropriate social institu-
        tions, can reach a high level of economic efficiency, meet
        consumer needs, and reconcile divergent social interests.

      • It will create a better foundation for establishing an effec-
        tive social safety net.

      • Only afterwards can Hungary hope to become integrated

into the Europe with which Hungary has been historically linked. If Hungary wishes to join the EC, which is a widely proclaimed political goal, it will have to have an economy based on principles acceptable and attractive to the EC.

International Experience and Its Relevance for Hungary

The Blue Ribbon Commission is aware that market economies do   30
not have uniform political aims, legal frameworks, or institutional arrangements. Therefore, the Commission does not wish to suggest what mixture of values Hungary's new government should adhere to. No single country is offered here as a "model." However, Hungary's location, traditions, and linkages suggest that particular attention needs to be paid to the European experience, without neglecting, in today's increasingly global world, the relevant experiences of other countries. Market economies that function well have certain common goals which are approached to a considerable degree. Some of them are set forth here:

- Continuous improvements of human and physical capital are encouraged. Individuals are motivated by the pressure of competition and the promise of reward to work up to their full potential.

- Money is stable and the financial system functions smoothly. People and enterprises have incentives to save, helping to provide the funds necessary for investment. Trustworthy financial intermediaries collect and channel savings through the capital market to their most productive uses. The credit standing of the country is sufficiently high to assure a steady flow of foreign capital, as needed.

- The state assumes some direct role, but the central government budget does not preempt too large a share of the economy's resources and aims for a reasonable balance. The aspirations of the people to make their country stronger and their lives more comfortable always exert strong pressure on a government to make its expenditures larger than the real strength of the economy can support. But responsible governments know that if a sound balance between the size and strength of the economy and the scope of the budget is not maintained, the inevitable result is inflation.

- The government is strong enough to resist pressure to maintain or increase subsidies as a seemingly easy way to solve difficult problems. Subsidies are like anodyne: they are sweet to those who receive them, but they undermine the functioning of the economy and impose burdens on everyone.

- The tax system provides sufficient revenue for the government, helps shape an income distribution that society considers fair, and does not impose a burden so high as to undermine the willingness to save, work, and be enterprising.

- The government, working with the private sector, invests in transportation, communications, and other infrastructure as an economic strategy to serve business sector and social aims alike.

- Free and fair competition is the rule rather than the exception; indeed, it is the essential mechanism that makes a market economy function well.

- Society provides an economic safety net--at a level society can afford and which does not discourage seeking employment--for all those who, for reasons beyond their control, are disadvantaged.

The Political Framework

31   The effective functioning of a market economy requires a high degree of trust by economic actors that their calculations can take

the important parameters of the economic system as given, and subject only to reasonably predictable incremental changes. A firm and consistent policy posture, informed by the overall direction and ultimate goals of the social, political, and economic transformation, is crucial to success. Creating the impression that the government is engaged in ad hoc maneuvering and muddling-through would entail high and long-lasting economic, political and social costs.

Society should be ruled by law, not by persons. Permanent laws   **32**
should spell out the basic rules in the economic marketplace, with special emphasis on property rights.

Central government should devolve as many governmental func-   **33**
tions as practical to independently elected local officials in order to keep government close to the people and accountable to them. An efficient local government will tend to reduce the heavy-handedness of the central bureaucracy and to foster local experimentation with alternate solutions to public problems.

The central government should allocate authority to local govern-   **34**
ment to pay for as much of local services as possible, through taxes (the authority for which must also be devolved) or by charging users fees for certain services. This will keep both taxing and spending authorities for local purposes close to the electorate concerned and accountable to it.

Other fundamental changes will be required in the structure and   **35**
processes of governing. In such areas as privatization, promoting entrepreneurship and small business, establishing efficient public administration, improving the educational and health systems, public utilities' regulation, and strengthening market institutions, the government needs to establish problem-solving procedures.

New programs will have to be designed to replace many old   **36**
benefits in order for the new economy to maintain its moral legitimacy. For example, the elimination of consumer subsidies and guaranteed employment will require partially offsetting welfare payments, unemployment compensation and job retraining pro-

grams, but these programs must fit the resources available and the social context.

37   Another feature of democratic life that will build support for the new government and its economic reform program is public hearings. In open meetings, officials of the new government should present their ideas to members of the public and ordinary citizens should be given a chance to express their own views. Advisory boards and elected officials alike find that the exchanges between citizens in public hearings can make a positive contribution to the thinking behind public policy development. Public hearings also have the effect of persuading the public that they can be heard by policymakers, whether or not the views expressed at such hearings are finally adopted.

38   The government should propose a "Freedom of Information" act that would enable citizens to have direct access to information in public institutions, such as ministries, government agencies, and state-owned enterprises. Limitations should not exceed the degree necessitated by the state's legitimate security interests and the need for preserving legitimate commercial secrets.

39   Freedom of speech contributes to public debate and understanding of the economy, as well as all other segments of life. It should not be restricted in any way except by a libel law to protect individuals from malicious slander disseminated in the media.

40   In restructuring government agencies, the new government should bear in mind both direct and indirect savings to be found in abolishing agencies which regulate the economy but have outlived their usefulness. Economic ministries will function best in the interest of an efficient economy if they are lean on personnel, with as few bureaucratic layers as possible. The government may wish to use some of the funds thus saved to support administration of new programs to effectuate privatization, education in small business creation, and consumer protection.

41   A council of economic advisors should be established, appointed by the Prime Minister and made up of members valued for their

independent and practical experience in the operation of market economies.

The new Civil Service will prove most economic and non-political   42
if retention of existing members is based on loyalty to the Republic
of Hungary (affirmed by oath); qualification by merit; proven job
performance; and a demonstrated need for continuation of the
given position itself.

Routine (non-discretionary) tasks should not be carried out through   43
political determination and should be handled by agencies, departments, and representative offices subordinated to the minister.

Principles of Economic Transition

Once a government has defined its objectives clearly, it must im-   44
plement change in quantum leaps. Reforms must be packaged into
large bundles because the economy operates as an organic whole,
not as an unrelated collection of bits and pieces. When reforms are
packaged into a large bundle, the linkages in the system can be
relied upon for each action to effectively enhance every other
action. Large packages will demonstrate that the losses suffered
by any one group are offset by gains in other areas.

Deciding on a quantum leap is also a matter of political efficiency.   45
Slowness can cause the early consensus supporting the government's program to collapse before implementation is completed
and results become evident, because interest groups have time to
mobilize and drag down the program. Requests from interest
groups for a slower pace often turn out, on closer analysis, to
represent fear that the government is not spreading the pain
equally.

A government need not have broad public support for each   46
specific reform measure. Seeking ex ante support for each measure leads to excessive compromise that emasculates a comprehensive program. Experience shows that political consensus develops

progressively once the decisions are made and satisfactory results are delivered to the public.

47   Concerning the pace of transformation, the place for caution is generally at the policy-deliberation phase. Extensive consideration should be given to alternatives, to the likelihood of achieving intended and unintended consequences, to sequencing, and to modes of implementation. However, it is the hope of the Blue Ribbon Commission that its work will make it possible for the new government to spend less time on this phase than would otherwise have been necessary. This is all the more important because the new government should announce and begin implementing its program quickly, while it enjoys a "honeymoon period" with the electorate. This is why the Commission has a separate set of recommendations on what the new government might wish to do during its (approximately) first 100 days in office.

48   We wish to underscore again that speed in implementing the program is essential. Any large program will take years to put into place even at maximum speed. The key is to provide a preannounced path, a clear sense of the new direction, and a firm timetable of the actions that will be taken. This will give the government time to prepare the implementation of its program and the economy's actors time to adjust to what they must be convinced are inevitable changes. West European integration by 1992 is a prime example. In this context, 1992 is not just a date but a process which began as soon as the goal was announced. The landing should therefore be "soft" because individuals, firms, and institutions will have had time to adjust to the rules that they know will go fully into effect by the preannounced date.

49   Public policy must be consistent and credible to generate economic confidence at home and abroad. The keys to credibility are high-quality decisions, consistency of actions, and communications with the public--telling the truth about the economic situation, showing how the government will deal with it and why the alternatives to the government's proposals are less attractive. Credibility also means not raising unrealistic expectations. If government policies lack credibility, people refuse to change their be-

havior to fit new policies and thus shackle the economy with psychological costs that otherwise could have been avoidable. Government policies that are not credible also will fail to generate the kind of external financial and political support needed to facilitate program implementation.

Public education about the timing of the program is vital. It would   **50**
not be prudent to promise that it is possible to find ways of correcting mistakes and distortions that have been accumulating for 45 years without causing pain during the early stages of the transformation. Shortages must be eliminated by allowing prices to rise, though this development should not be allowed to cascade into permanent inflation. Structural adjustment will involve significant unemployment but this should be partly temporary if free enterprise during the transformation can grow fast enough to absorb the resources liberated from the shrinking state sector. Therefore, the fact that there is pain should not be an indication of the failure of the transformation program, but rather that the program may indeed be effective. If the transformation is not attempted fully or is allowed to falter, then the entire country and each interest group within it will be worse off and decline will not easily be arrested. Speedy transformation is the only way, even though it will take time before sustained recovery gathers momentum. Certain benefits of the transformation program should be apparent within months--for example, the improved quality and availability of consumer goods and services; cuts in waste and inefficiency; and better employment opportunities for skilled, diligent, and reliable employees. Substantial benefits will be enjoyed first by a small segment of society (mainly the entrepreneurs); but in time, broader and broader segments will benefit.

Chapter 2

PROMOTING ENTREPRENEURSHIP AND TRANSFORMING OWNERSHIP

The Current Situation

51   No modern economy can function well or generate sustained improvement in the standard of living if private ownership of the means of production is not predominant. Private property has been found to be an indispensable, though by itself insufficient, condition of political democracy as well as economic progress. Politically, diversified centers of power and decision-making must be created to ensure the growth and maintenance of true democracy. Economically, efficient markets must be created to deliver the better quality of life that the citizens demand and deserve.

52   The new Hungarian government faces several interrelated problems relating to ownership. One is how to promote the establishment and growth of small businesses, primarily in the private sector, in order to create networks of suppliers and service establishments that are now largely missing in the economy; to spark creative competition; and to provide new opportunities for employment. Another is how to privatize quickly and efficiently a significant number of existing state enterprises and make them more efficient. A connected challenge is to improve the efficiency of enterprises that permanently or temporarily will remain state-

owned. If the transformation is to succeed, each of these problems must be given high priority attention and solved together.

In section A of this chapter, we discuss the BRC recommendations   53
on entrepreneurship, and in section B, on privatization and related
issues.

A. Promoting Entrepreneurship

Rationale

Entrepreneurship--which here we use in the limited sense of   54
starting new private or genuinely cooperative businesses or expanding existing ones--plays an essential role in Hungary's transition to a new and productive economy. Entrepreneurs:

- generate competition, without which the market does not
  function well;

- provide substantial new employment, which in Hungary
  will mean absorbing new entrants to the labor force as
  well as many of those who will be laid off in the declining
  sectors;

- most energetically advance innovation and improvements
  in products and services, and thereby enhance consumer
  welfare.

Legacies

Today, the private entrepreneurial sector is small and undercapi-   55
talized, operating mainly in fields that demand little capital. At
least half of the entrepreneurs are able to pursue their activities
part time, while holding down a job in the state or cooperative
sector.

The rapid development of the private sector is constrained by   56
several factors. Investment of personal funds, whether one's own

funds or those of families or friends, which in market economies often is the most common capital source for new businesses, is made difficult in Hungary, where savings of the average person are low and are not increasing. What savings exist are typically not invested in domestic business but seek more "secure" opportunities, such as foreign currency or real estate, which does not particularly help overall economic growth.

57   The most binding constraint is access to finance. At present, the Hungarian banking system is poorly adapted to provide financing because the economy is dominated by a very few large banks that pay little attention to small business. At the same time, most of the two dozen or so small banks lack enough financial resources to help set up new businesses.

58   Bureaucratic obstacles, namely, compliance with central and local rules and regulations, are still extensive. The tax burden on entrepreneurs is high. Business rental property is scarce and expensive.

Recommendations

59   The new government should take the following steps:

- Pledge its highest priority attention to making the existence of the private business sector politically and economically secure.

- Enter into immediate negotiations with the association(s) representing private business on ways to change the tax system in line with the recommendations made in Chapter 4.

- Renovate unutilized industrial plants for use by new businesses, in close cooperation with local government organs. The facilities should be made available at market-determined rents.

- Pledge that it regularly will devote a certain portion of

state revenues obtained from the privatization of state property to promote entrepreneurs.

- Make sure that the minimum size of the financing pool made available for start-up loans to unemployed persons who would like to open new businesses is not eroded by inflation.

- Provide preferential treatment in start-up capital and credit. Instruments may include venture capital funds, special bonds for small business firms and credit pools established with substantial state contributions. Provide loan guarantees for those would-be entrepreneurs who do not as yet have sufficient wealth to provide collateral, on the condition that the lender and the entrepreneur also share in the risk.

- Promote the development of a financial system that is capable of adjusting to the life cycle, size, and riskiness of new business ventures. Give banks incentives to establish a department or unit to deal exclusively with small business; open up the economy to the inflow of venture capital.

- Appoint a sub-cabinet-level government official for small business who is to report to the government and Parliament regularly on the problems and accomplishments of small businesses.

- Encourage the educational system to develop and use training courses for entrepreneurship. Schools should create links with entrepreneurial groups. Educational institutions also should provide opportunities for students to be exposed first-hand to the entrepreneurial experience (e.g., organizing school cooperatives and mini-businesses).

- Assure that support for starting or expanding private businesses does not come exclusively or even mainly from the central government, but develops individually and locally, in all kinds of ways. Locally-organized business services should provide information, marketing and accounting support, advice on how to set up business plans, where to apply for credit, and the like.

- Enact a package of laws removing discrimination against entrepreneurial and small businesses in regulations and licensing.

- Monitor continuously the financial regulators and the administrative environment in which they operate to find out what kinds of burdens and costs are being imposed on entrepreneurs.

- Prepare an operating manual for entrepreneurs which summarizes all that a person needs to know to start and operate a business. Special attention should be paid to the legal, tax, bookkeeping and cost-accountancy aspects. Special permits that may be required should be noted. The manual should encourage entrepreneurs to evaluate continually their financial situation, to facilitate their negotiations with financial institutions.

B. Privatization

Rationale

60   There are no proven means to motivate producers toward efficiency, customer satisfaction, and innovative behavior in societies where the state owns most assets and does not allow genuine markets to develop. Private enterprise, subject to competition and rules, will improve:

- productive efficiency, because competition reverses state-owned firms' insufficient motivation to hold costs down and care for the value of assets (much of the consequent gain will then be passed on to consumers through lower prices);

- allocative efficiency, because competition and the profit motive will stimulate producers to supply the kinds of goods and services that consumers actually want, and to deliver them at the times and places that are convenient for the buyers; and

- innovative efficiency, because the pressure of competition and the opportunity of financial gain will provide crucially important motivation for research and development, innovation, and new product development.

A further argument for privatization is its role in creating a market   61
environment and promoting competition. Competition cannot be decreed or centrally organized; it must emerge as the natural behavior of many parties pursuing their self-interest, within a framework that does not condone abuses. With private ownership typically come higher profits and thus a better long-term basis for business expansion, creation of new jobs, and improvement of goods and services, at lower prices. At the same time differences in incomes and wealth will increase.

Privatization yields public sector as well as private benefits be-   62
cause it limits the scope of political interference with economic decisions. It increases financial discipline on firms because it eliminates--or at least diminishes--the expectation of direct financial support from the government, especially official protection from competition. Once privatized, moreover, enterprises which in the past may have lost revenue for the state can be taxed, contributing revenue to the state that can be used for general purposes.

Situation Inherited

State enterprises and large cooperatives provide more than two-   63
thirds of industrial production; they own an even larger share of total industrial assets. Industrial organization, even after the introduction of the New Economic Mechanism ("NEM") in 1968, has remained highly concentrated. Hungary lacks a well-developed medium- and small-scale industrial and trade sector, which

in most countries would provide many of the inputs and services that Hungarian enterprises now produce internally and inefficiently, if at all.

64   The 1984-85 reforms established enterprise councils in the majority of state-owned Hungarian firms, and transferred many of the (not always clearly defined) ownership rights to the councils. In spite of expectations, this did not improve economic efficiency. Though management and employees supposedly have 50-50 representation, the managers typically have had the dominant voice. At the end of 1988 this kind of enterprise council "ownership" characterized approximately 2000 of the 2800 state-owned enterprises. But since enterprises remaining in state ownership are of larger size, on average, the total value of industrial production and assets of firms "owned" by enterprise councils and the total value of those owned by the state are roughly equivalent.

65   The Company Law (1988) and, to a lesser extent, the Law on Transformation (1989), have made it possible to develop new types of enterprises, such as subsidiaries, joint ventures, and joint stock and limited liability companies.

66   In January 1990, Parliament passed the Law on Protection of Property Entrusted to State Enterprises. The law founded the State Property Agency (SPA), which became operational on March 1, 1990.

67   The SPA, under the law, was placed directly under Parliament. Its task is to monitor the privatization process; in some cases initiating it, in others simply making sure that the rules are followed, even though the initiative to privatize comes from the enterprise itself. In the former cases, the decision about privatization is made by the SPA under parliamentary guidelines. In all other cases, privatization does not need a special state decision but can proceed "spontaneously," so long as it is consistent with the legislation. Let's call firms in the first group "strategic" enterprises and in the second group, "other" enterprises. (Below, the BRC makes separate sets of recommendations on how privatization should proceed in each of these two categories.)

Regrettably, the partial change of state ownership to self-manage-   68
ment in the mid-1980s and the early rules and steps that permitted
half-hearted privatization have become obstacles to a more comprehensive and economically sound transformation of ownership.
Privatization, as it proceeded in 1989 and early 1990, had several
undesirable features that have created a wholly justified negative
reaction. Those include the following:

- When enterprise councils gained the right to sell an enterprise, there was nothing to prohibit negotiation for large
  and possibly unearned personal gains ("golden para-
  chutes") for the old management.

- Practically no revenue accrued to the state from the sale of
  assets arising from privatization, since the ownership
  shares remained with the company.

- The financial records of state enterprises did not meet
  international standards, making valuation of these enterprises extremely difficult. This is one reason that the
  liabilities of the firms or units being privatized were often
  not properly handled.

- The law did not insist that the privatizing enterprise
  should be sold competitively, and thus properly valued,
  nor that the transaction be fully transparent, which would
  have permitted public scrutiny.

- In many cases, the transformation of an enterprise into a
  company did not represent real change, did not really
  promote the creation of a genuinely new ownership structure, but was simply a pseudo-transformation to enable
  the enterprise to continue doing business as before, but
  under a "modern" label.

- The law granted different tax favors to foreign investors
  in all sectors, thus placing Hungarian enterprises at a
  competitive disadvantage.

69   There are several other problems that a new strategy of privatization will have to take into consideration:

- Most businesses will require considerable restructuring before or after sale, since they typically are over-staffed, lack modern production and marketing expertise, and cannot raise sufficient capital for expansion in the presently underdeveloped domestic capital market.

- Another difficulty is that production and distribution are both heavily centralized. Many sectors are dominated by monopolies or oligopolies. Accordingly, it is necessary to consider the effects of each privatization on future competition and on consumer prices.

70   In the financial services sector, Hungarian banking is poorly adapted to requirements for efficient financial intermediation. Money and capital markets and institutions are notably underdeveloped. The existing sector, moreover, is dominated by a few large banks which possess many non-performing assets and are not impelled to foreclose on the debtors. The present financial institutions are also short of needed professional and technical skills.

71   In housing, the present ownership patterns and methods of finance are economically inefficient and socially unjust (see Chapter 6). In this chapter we wish to note only that the state agencies that own much of the housing in the urban areas have not even been able to cover their operating expenses; that maintenance standards have declined; that the housing stock is steadily deteriorating; and that the housing shortage remains serious.

72   Other infrastructure, until now, has not been affected by reform. The overwhelming share of public utilities and all public transport, pipelines, and communications systems are government monopolies, and all development decisions are made by the center.

Recommendations

The fundamental objective of transforming ownership is the whole-   73
sale transfer of most state assets to new owners, who, with the
rights of ownership and by interests in dividends and capital
gains, will improve the utilization of those assets.

The overall privatization process must maintain a sense of ur-   74
gency and momentum, though, of course, it should not set unrealistic targets or deadlines that create a sense of panic or failure.
This implies a deliberate and rapid process, with few limitations as
to sector or size. In three years at least one-third of presently state-
owned enterprises should be in private hands, and in five years at
least one-half. Privatization should focus both on enterprises that
do not pose difficult problems, and in which the expected return
on capital is high, and on firms facing special difficulties, such as
having to reorient their trade from the CMEA to the world market.

As background for the BRC's recommendations on how the priva-   75
tization should be financed and the proceeds used, let us note that

- the book value of all state-owned enterprises is about
  2,000 billion Hungarian forints (about $30 billion);

- the current annual flow of private currency savings that
  could be available for purchasing assets (other than real
  estate) is not more than 20 billion HUF (about $300 mil-
  lion) per year;

- the government's domestic debt is about 1,200 billion
  HUF (about $15 billion);

- the National Bank of Hungary's foreign debt is about
  1,400 billion HUF (about $20 billion);

- the annual flow of foreign direct investment in 1989 was
  about $300 million (about 20 billion HUF).

76   These figures show that at the present rate of domestic savings, it would take Hungarians a hundred years to purchase all state enterprises.

77   So, in addition to efforts to import capital for economic growth (as described below and in Chapter 5), the new Hungarian government needs to find additional ways to expand the potential for increasing domestic Hungarian ownership of privatized assets.

78   We recommend that privatization should be supported by a special line of credit, to be made available only to the citizens of Hungary, and to be used only for buying equities. How much this will speed domestic privatization will depend largely on the margin requirements; i.e., the percent of the purchase price that the domestic buyer will be required to put down as a condition of obtaining credit. An important goal in this scheme should be sales to workers, helped by preferential credit facilities or as a quid pro quo for productivity improvements.

79   Rapid privatization implies that there also will have to be large sales and/or placements to pension funds, mutual funds, nonprofit foundations, local governments, insurance companies, and similar organizations. Thus, privatization needs to be supported by the rapid development of financial intermediaries.

80   But even maximized domestic investments cannot fully capitalize the transformation of Hungary into a modern economy. The objective of privatization reinforces all the other reasons why significant amounts of new capital should be imported by sales of assets or equities to foreigners. Some critics may object to what they see as the "sale of Hungary's destiny to outsiders." At one time or another that largely mistaken fear is heard in nearly every country. But, if heeded, it will lead to a poorer economy, not a more secure one. Studies of successfully growing modern economies show that they almost always import large shares of capital and with it, just as importantly, large amounts of technology and managerial, professional, and technical know-how. (See discussion on Foreign Direct Investment, "FDI", in Chapter 5.)

The government's revenues from privatization (outright sales,   81
down payments and debt service) should be used to reduce the
government's domestic and foreign debt, and as contributions to
a revolving fund to provide credits for the start-up of new private
business ventures and expansions. Under no circumstances should
the revenues be used to help cover current government expenditures because that would be inflationary. Regular expenses must
be covered from regular revenue sources.

The present law, which subordinates privatization strategy and   82
supervision directly to Parliament, is not a prudent arrangement.
The way privatization is carried out affects a whole range of
economic programs and thus should be integrated with them.
Such integration can be managed only by the government. Parliament should set broad guidelines and monitor their implementation, but should not have direct responsibility for privatization.
Moreover, since privatization must balance a complex set of
national priorities, and ministries typically have only single mis-
sions (e.g., maximizing revenue), the new privatization agency
must be self-standing within the government. This will give privatization the focused high priority it requires.

To increase the financial discipline of state enterprises, the state   83
must take the following steps:

- Impose on them a "rate of return on equity" charge. This
  obligation should replace the present "special" corporate
  tax. The real value of each enterprise's assets has to be
  negotiated between the enterprise and the state.

- Tighten and enforce more vigorously the bankruptcy law.

- Reorganize the operation of the banking system. Loan
  portfolios must be cleansed of those non-performing loans
  that were handed to the banks in 1987 when the banks
  were created. Immediately thereafter, banks should be
  required to try to collect from enterprises all other debt-
  service obligations that are due. This will increase financial discipline on firms and also on banks, thus promoting
  competition in domestic banking.

84   The new government might consider ways to promote a system in which deposit-taking (commercial or merchant) banks' and investment banks' activities are regulated differently, since deposit-taking banks are more strictly controlled. The investment banks should play an important role in the transformation of insolvent firms into creditworthy ones via privatization. The investment banks could perform this task themselves or contract it out to profit-making institutions, domestic or foreign. Before privatization, the organizations that will "sanitize" the non-performing loans should negotiate with the privatization agency the price at which the latter will "purchase" these loans, using the proceeds of earlier privatizations.

85   For the group of enterprises we call "strategic," the state already exercises ownership and control functions. The BRC recommends that, for this group of enterprises, the Ministry of Finance and other competent authorities set up an "interagency privatization working group," with responsibility to supervise the particular transaction. Control of the process should remain with the interagency working group (i.e., with the government) rather than with the enterprise to be privatized because, on a number of issues, the objectives of the firm will be in conflict with the interests of the state.

86   The financial/legal/accounting consultants involved in the transaction should be retained and paid by the government and not by the enterprise to be privatized, in order to avoid their being "captured" by management of the firm being privatized.

87   For "other" firms, the state is the effective owner, but ownership functions are exercised by enterprise councils. If and when such "other" enterprises are to be privatized--whether by self-initiation, or as the result of bankruptcy proceedings, or when triggered by a firm's inability to meet its financial obligations--a new law should provide that ownership functions in the sale or reorganization will be exercised by a state agency, which need not necessarily be the SPA. The logic of this proposed law is that, if the sale yields net proceeds, those should go to the state, just as, if liabilities are greater than assets, the state should have the responsibility to absorb the losses.

The key to good procedures is competition between prospective   **88**
buyers and sellers. Only this can ensure proper valuation.

In all cases, a framework law should be enacted, stipulating: **89**

- how to maintain or re-establish the state's fiduciary interest in the assets and liabilities of these enterprises;

- basic rules governing the transparency of any sale of
  enterprises (e.g. advertisement of any sale, due notice,
  method of auction, etc.); and

- powers granted to the SPA to veto or suspend any transaction not conforming to the basic rules.

Hungary's privatization priorities and rules should be clearly   **90**
stated. The process must be well understood by all players. The
new government should guarantee a stable legislative framework.

To establish a privatization process that is fully transparent and   **91**
thereby reduce the chances of "inside deals," the following multi-
layered approach (based on contracts between the state organs
mentioned in paragraph 85 and private companies) is proposed:

- First, an independent and qualified private company
  (domestic, foreign or joint Hungarian-foreign) should
  evaluate each enterprise to be privatized, prepare a prospectus that discloses full information about the business,
  and advise the agency or financial institution in charge of
  privatization about how it should proceed.

- Next, another fully independent company, such as an
  investment bank, should be retained to seek prospective
  buyers and negotiate the sale.

- Finally, the government agency that is accountable for
  assuring conformance with Parliamentary guidelines
  should prepare periodic reports to Parliament and de-
  fend its record in open hearings.

92   Negotiations on privatization should involve the employees and management of the firm to be privatized, though employees should not have a veto. Different types of employee ownership arrangements should be available as options to be negotiated if there is mutual (owner and employee) interest.

93   Practically all retail trade, service establishments, workshops, and similar units of firms (if they can be partitioned) should be privatized within one year by employing sector-specific approaches. This recommendation means that parent companies should be forced to sell their outlets and shops to private buyers who will obtain real assets in exchange for cash and real payment obligations. Special steps must also be taken in wholesale trade. The purpose of privatization in these branches, besides all the usual objectives, is to deconcentrate monopolistic and oligopolistic activities.

94   In agriculture, the principles of voluntary participation in cooperatives and the desire to return to a constitutionally protected system of private ownership have given rise to a demand for revision of the present ownership structure. What sets apart the situation in this sector is the fact that even today about 40% of the cooperatives' land is still the legal property of individual members, even though they are unable to dispose of its use. Another large number of cooperative members are previous owners, who were forced to "sell" their land.

95   A new Act on Agricultural Land has to be enacted. The first object of the law is to guarantee the right of private ownership of land and the right to dispose of land to those having preserved land ownership to the present day, including those whose land is used by the cooperatives. Land transferred earlier to the cooperatives, or similar land, should be offered for repurchase to the original owners at a preferential price. (Some members of the BRC also would include the original owners' heirs if they are ready to cultivate it.) A free market for land should be established, subject to certain restrictions (e.g., on availability to foreign owners for certain types of uses).

The BRC recommends, further, that the following principles guide   **96**
the decisions of the new government on land ownership reform:

- Transformation should favor the interest of those individuals who wish to acquire land for agricultural rather
  than other pursuits, and their farming activities should be
  supported.

- Transformation should not threaten even the temporary
  drop of agricultural production.

- Transformation should dissolve the local monopoly of
  collective and state farms over land resources in their area
  and put pressure on collective farms to discontinue economically wasteful practices.

Details of the land ownership transformation should be decided   **97**
and implemented at the local level, taking into account the sum
total of land claims. If no voluntary agreement can be reached
between the claimants and the collective and the state farms, the
law should provide for compulsory arbitration.

Community ownership of pastures and woodlands should be re-   **98**
stored.

Regarding ownership reform in housing (discussed in Chapter 6),   **99**
the current process of privatizing state-owned flats should continue.

In infrastructure, too, there should be a program of deregulation,   **100**
together with the establishment of a new legal and institutional
framework that will make possible and promote privatization.
The central government should retain broad planning responsibility for the railroad system and for the national networks; i.e., the
main roads, the oil and gas pipelines, the electricity grid, the
waterways, and the telephone system. But it should look for
innovative ways of cooperating with the private sector to finance,
build, and operate the needed investments. This is especially
important in telecommunications, but also in such other areas as

turnpikes (e.g., Vienna-Budapest) and building new capacity to generate electricity. Local infrastructure, including tie-in networks, should be the responsibility of the municipalities, together with new budget authority. Thereafter, the population in each area should decide development priorities and their financing.

Chapter 3

BUILDING THE INSTITUTIONAL FRAMEWORK FOR THE MARKET

Legacies

101   In Hungary since 1968 the state and the market theoretically coexist and jointly determine resource allocation, but until now the tradition of central direction of the economy has remained dominant. Moreover, still in effect are many administrative rules and financial regulators that distort market forces and hinder the adaptability of enterprises and households to the requirements of a modern economic system.

Tasks

102   The transformation of the economic system requires prompt establishment of an economic, financial, and legal framework that fully allows the development of market forces and the evolution of a vibrant private sector.

103   Paradoxically, although in a market economy central authority will play a much smaller role than it did in the communist system, Parliament must now endow the newly chosen government with rather sweeping powers to carry out the transition. Parliament can legislate and supervise; but it cannot execute, especially when there is so much to be done in such a short period of time. During the reform period, any step that weakened central authority was

widely considered a step in the right direction. Today, after the election of a truly representative Parliament, that perspective temporarily must be suspended.

The complete withdrawal of the state from the economy during   104
the transformation process would increase uncertainty both at home and abroad, and reduce the chances for success in the short and long term. Government has a role to play. Its aim must be to replace policies that control and direct with policies that enable all actors and sectors to adapt to new domestic and international circumstances. In some instances, it may also be necessary for the state to stimulate or restrict certain economic activities.

Thus, a major task of the new government is to establish an insti-   105
tutional framework for the market. The principles and recommendations of how this should be done are summarized below, separately for each main area.

Creating and Maintaining Competition

Free competition is the most essential building block of a well-   106
functioning market economy. Competition policy should be based on freedom to acquire property as declared by law, freedom of business activity, freedom of entry into and exit from the market, and free labor mobility.

The high degree of monopolization in the Hungarian economy is   107
an obstacle to establishing competition as a force for increasing efficiency. The government should direct a four-pronged attack against monopolies to create and maintain free competition.

First, because rapid growth in the number and diversity of market   108
participants is needed, the establishment and promotion of small and medium-size enterprises, including voluntary cooperatives, should be supported by a complete range of measures and policies (see the previous chapter). To promote competition, all legal and administrative restrictions hindering it must be removed quickly.

109   Second, import competition should be utilized fully to increase the efficiency and competitiveness of all economic units.

110   Third, the new government should design and implement a program of deconcentration, breaking up monopolies where technical and economic considerations suggest and where import competition is weak or absent. During 1989 the artificially high concentration of the economy decreased as the number of industrial enterprises increased by over 50%. Further deconcentration programs should be undertaken in industry, agriculture, construction, transportation, trade, and the other service sectors.

111   Fourth, the norms of unfair competition should be clearly established and enforced. An office of competition and antitrust should create and enforce a legal framework for the effective functioning of a competitive marketplace. Natural monopolies, such as public utilities, must be regulated. Intervention by the office of competition and antitrust should be guided by the concept of "market domination," which asks: Do suppliers and buyers have viable domestic or international alternatives? If not, under this policy, there should be strong presumption that competition is unfair. In such situations especially, the law should prohibit the imposition of "exclusive dealing," "resale price maintenance," and various predatory pricing practices. "Insider trading," where people with access to privileged information exploit it to their unfair personal economic advantage in the market, should be prohibited and policed.

112   A great deal of attention should be paid to cartel agreements or cartel-like networking among firms producing similar products or close substitutes. An agency should monitor and prevent anticompetitive behavior. Hungary's new government may wish to review the laws and practices of other countries in this area, adapting whatever might be appropriate for Hungarian conditions.

Pricing

Today, the government still influences prices through several   **113**
mechanisms. In the area of producer prices, there are compulsory
rules of price formation for energy and raw materials, which
means that prevailing world market prices are charged, justifia-
bly, irrespective of the actual cost of production or the acquisition
price from CMEA sources. In agriculture, there is a complex
system of intervention, one element of which is setting minimum
or maximum prices for certain products. Prices set by public
utilities and those of several other products (e.g. automobiles,
milk, and bread) are administratively controlled. And in areas of
activity where producers have a monopoly, the intention to raise
prices must be reported to the Price Office, which may require
some sort of an explanation or justification. Price liberalization in
these areas should proceed as quickly as the development of
competition allows.

The process of price liberalization should be continued. As a rule,   **114**
prices should be set by market forces. State intervention must be
limited to situations in which compelling economic or social
reasons require it.

The prices charged by public utilities should cover costs and be   **115**
supervised.

To increase competition, procurement on the part of state and local   **116**
governments should be done under international competitive
bidding.

Market for Goods and Non-Financial Services

Role of the Government

In a market economy, the central government plays a very differ-   **117**
ent role in relation to the marketplace than under the previous
system. In most cases, the central government should not be a
player but the referee. Private enterprise, acting through the

mechanism of the marketplace, should provide most of the goods and services. Areas such as transport, communications, banking, garbage collection, medical services, and education should not be government monopolies. Free entry should be allowed, leaving open the possibility that private enterprise will eventually take over fully some of these sectors. Government may in various ways control, aid, or subsidize the delivery of the goods and services through direct grants, tax credits, and regulations, although such interference should remain limited so as not to distort market forces unduly.

118   There is no need for the government to establish sector-specific industrial development projects. Instead, it can promote certain economic policy objectives by supporting basic research, maintaining good educational and information systems, improving infrastructure, and pursuing sound policies at the macro level. The number of priorities and extent of preferences should remain limited, again, so as not to unduly distort market forces.

Research and Development

119   Concerning Research and Development:

- It is necessary to support the professional work and foreign training of Hungarian researchers and experts, as well the activity of foreign researchers, university educators, and engineers in Hungary.

- It is essential to develop the real autonomy of basic research institutions and universities.

- Technological and R&D institutions should be transformed into companies and operated as profit-oriented business ventures, open to foreign participation.

- The new government should define a new national technology policy. The number of priorities should be limited. Among them should be such goals as integrating Hungary into the technological processes of developed coun-

tries in the applications of electronics and advanced information systems, biotechnology, and environmental protection.

Infrastructure

Concerning infrastructure, a significant part of it should be decon-   **120**
centrated and deregulated, as recommended in Chapter 2. Development priority should be given to:

- telecommunications, where the new government should
  choose quickly one from among several proposals as to
  which form the deregulation and development strategy
  should take (all options now being considered are recom-
  mending that the private sector, including foreign investors, should play a predominant role);

- the road and turnpike network, where the new government should determine and implement a long-term development and financing strategy, again with the participation of foreign investors;

- tourist facilities, which may require an incentive program
  for the private sector.

Not only philosophical but practical considerations suggest that   **121**
infrastructure should be opened up to foreign investment: the
central budget is simply not in a position to devote the resources
needed to develop and maintain this important sector at the
desired level of efficiency.

Agriculture

In agriculture, while the satisfaction of traditional domestic demand   **122**
ought to be a constant goal, further development of export markets for non-traditional and value-added agricultural products
should be fostered through development of flexible policies related to the gathering and dissemination of market information,
R&D, experimental activities, and export promotion.   Policies

need to be developed separately for the near future and for the medium- and long-run. For example, during the difficult transition period, the economy will not be able to do without the export earnings from agriculture. Thus, some minimum government support in the face of a highly protected and distorted world market may be necessary. Some members stressed that even this limited support may be avoided if the exchange rate is set by market forces, as this group recommends elsewhere in this report.

123 In addition, the state could play a useful supporting role in the transition to voluntary cooperatives and independent farming. This will require a reorientation of the supporting institutional infrastructure--including those elements that deal with R&D and technological change--from large to small- and medium-scale operations, and from services provided to state and collective organizations to a mix in which private enterprises play an increasing role.

124 Further attention is needed to the specific credit needs of agricultural entrepreneurs in production, in input services, and in processing and marketing. Agricultural education should receive a new boost by increased participation of agrarian self-help organizations. Its orientation should be on economic skill and entrepreneurial functions.

Consumer Affairs

125 To increase consumer consciousness, the new government should adopt a declaration of consumer rights, including the right to choose, the right to be informed, the right to be heard, and the right to be safe. The declaration should be supported by legislation specifying the legal provisions concerning consumer protection, health and technical safety requirements, and the mechanism of enforcement.

Labor Market

The government should promote labor market conditions in which   **126**
the creation of new jobs and not the protection of existing jobs is
paramount, and under which high employment and not full
employment is the goal.

Employers in both the private and public sectors should be free to   **127**
decide the optimum number of employees on the basis of efficiency. Unless a significant number of workers are released from
economically unproductive pursuits, there can be no restructuring of the economy, there will be insufficient human and physical
resources to transfer to the many areas that need to be expanded,
work discipline will not improve, and wage-push inflation will be
substantial.

As a result of restructuring, human resources will be reallocated   **128**
from the state to the private sector, from large to small- and
medium-sized enterprises, and from manufacturing to service
industries. This, however, cannot happen without occupational
and geographic mobility and a significantly improved "social
safety net" for workers who temporarily lose jobs. The institutions and measures now in place in Hungary to assist workers
with the transition from one job to another and from employment
to retirement are simply inadequate to serve workers in a modern
market economy, much less to meet their needs during the up-
heaval that will be caused by the transition from a centrally directed to a market economy.

Making the labor market more flexible requires eliminating legal   **129**
and financial restrictions on such matters as enterprise- or unit-
specific reductions in working hours, temporary and part-time
work, and job classifications. Legislation and collective agreements should provide a framework for flexible and legally clear-
cut practices on layoffs.

Policies should differentiate between unemployment and welfare   **130**
benefits and promote the development of a "social safety net"
which recognizes this distinction. To put such policies into place,

a clear operational definition of "unemployed" must be developed: those who are without employment (work for pay less than a given number of hours per week) and are actively seeking employment. The "social safety net" should include unemployment compensation that is limited in time, employment services geared to finding new jobs, and retraining for tomorrow's jobs.

131   To mitigate potential unemployment, policies and regulations restricting self-employment activities should be removed.

132   Crisis and structural transformation have a particularly strong effect upon certain regions: the mining villages, the metallurgical towns, and certain backward agricultural regions. Direct government support to hard-hit regions should be restricted to a small number of the areas with the highest unemployment rate.

133   The new labor market requires an effective framework of labor relations for the public and private sectors. Privatization not only creates a new type of ownership but also generates a new category of "private employees" whose interests must also be protected. Thus, the development of a system protecting individual workers' rights needs to be constructed, together with arrangements for the protection of the rights of employers. This should be done through the establishment of a non-political and non-governmental dispute-resolution mechanism, involving arbitration, mediation, and other standard techniques employed in the industrialized countries. Successful employee grievance-handling techniques and some form of employee participation at the workplace have been demonstrated to improve employee morale, productivity, and innovation.

134   The government should promote an occupational safety and health code that adequately protects workers and does not put employers at a competitive disadvantage. It also should facilitate the creation of a continuing education system that would allow adults to prepare themselves over time for career changes. The vocational education system should provide training not of narrow specialists but of workers with broad skills who, unlike the current generation of workers, can be retrained fairly easily in response to domestic and global economic changes.

Capital Market

Today, savings in Hungary are low and much of the savings pool   135
is not intermediated. The financial system and its instruments
need to be developed further, competition assured, and a sound
regulatory framework created.

As privatization develops, the equity and debt of such newly pri-   136
vatized firms would widen and deepen the capital (bond, stock
and other financial) markets. One of the main bases for the
development of capital markets must be liberalized dealing in
government debt. Issuance of new kinds of securities and money-
market instruments should be encouraged.

As the transformation proceeds, it will be important to weaken the   137
monopoly positions of the relatively few large commercial banks
and to further develop the network of small banks and other
financial institutions. Banking and financial services should be
open to foreign entry. This does not mean that each and every
Hungarian bank should be purchasable by foreign buyers. But
ways must be found to increase the number, the strength, and the
role of domestic and foreign financial intermediaries.

Hungary needs to develop a framework of regulation within   138
which the liberalized financial markets can work efficiently. Such
a regulatory system may be the responsibility of the central bank
or possibly that of an independent inspectorate that is not under
the direct control of the government. The regulatory framework
should include:

- standards of accounting, disclosure, and reporting;

- requirements to make markets either as primary or secon-
  dary dealers;

- conditions and legal requirements of financial instruments;

- non-discriminating entry conditions for all financial markets,
  including entry of foreign institutions;

- supervision of capital markets (the stock market is important, but until there is transparent accounting, valuation, and insider-trading-prevention systems, regulations should guard especially against speculative trading).

Environment

139   The external costs of business operations on the environment are often not treated adequately as part of the market economic calculus. The state has a valid and important role to play in this area.

140   The constitution should contain a statement on the need to preserve the environment for its short- and long-run benefits to people and give the state the power to enact the legislation deemed necessary to achieve this goal.

141   The new government should employ a set of market instruments, such as "pollution charges"--based on the principle that the polluter pays--to attack the problem of environmental degradation.

142   A closer study should be made of West European legislation and experience concerning the environment, with a view toward close cooperation with the environmental agencies of the EC countries. Furthermore, diplomatic steps should be taken to moderate the considerable amount of pollution coming from the neighboring non-EC countries, and initiating the regional coordination of environmental policies.

143   A major campaign should be mounted to encourage the public to understand and support government action on the environment. Public education also can help individuals learn to prevent environmental damage through a myriad of personal actions and through voluntary social action campaigns.

Chapter 4

CREATING MACROECONOMIC STABILITY

The Current Situation

144   The economy has suffered from disequilibrium since at least the 1973 world energy crisis. Hungary's economic system does not motivate producers to adapt the structure of production nor to become demand-oriented. Disequilibrium is especially pronounced in the balance of payments where the pressures are approaching crisis proportions. Monetary policy has not been an effective tool of macroeconomic management, partly because financial discipline on state-owned enterprises is weak, and also because the institutions of central and commercial banking are underdeveloped. Money does not fully integrate the economy.

145   Government debt exceeds 55% of GDP. The budget redistributes too large a share of the national income. In 1988, subsidies alone represented about 13% of GDP. The tax system, in principle, is modern, but it provides insufficient incentives for savings and the tax rates are too high. Since 1987, Hungary has had a separate central and commercial banking system, but the latter is oligopolistic. It lacks an appropriate level of reserves and a large share of its assets are of dubious quality or are outright non-performing.

146   Inflationary pressures have accelerated, as has open inflation. The increase in the price level targeted by the government for 1990 is around 20%.

Monetary Policy

Partly in response to pressure from the IMF, monetary authorities   **147**
have in recent years attempted to pursue a tight monetary policy.
The National Bank of Hungary succeeded quite well in controlling
the money supply, but only if "money supply" is defined nar-
rowly.

The tight monetary policy contributes to a phenomenon among   **148**
enterprises known as "queuing," which is an unofficial source of
mostly non-interest-bearing credit beyond the control of the government. This pool of pseudo-credit is a dangerous uncertain
quantity in any calculation of how to transform monetary policy.
In Hungary today, when enterprises cannot get direct financing,
they can post a bookkeeping gain by "selling" on credit to another
enterprise and with the intention of drawing on that credit at state
controlled banks. In reality, the second enterprise may be unable
to pay for the sale, but itself is engaged in demanding the same
kind of pseudo credit from its own customers, and so, on down the
line (or "queue"). In some cases, there is not even a market for the
goods "sold" and, in fact, it is not even clear that goods actually
may ever change hands. Economists are anything but certain how
much pseudo-credit is in the "queue," or credit pipeline, but it is
estimated at 20-25% of all enterprise credit.

Enterprises perhaps grant each other "involuntary credit" be-   **149**
cause they think they have no choice, depending as they do on only
a few large state-enterprise customers. Enterprises face an environment notable for arbitrary costs, prices, restrictions, regulations, "requests" (that can't be refused), and supply constraints.

But, if some of the queuing is built into the system, some is largely   **150**
exploitative on the part of certain managers, since there is little
incentive in law or regulation to avoid the temptation to manipu-
late the opportunities for "involuntary credit."

Many enterprises also are in a monopoly or oligopoly situation,   **151**
which makes it difficult to move against them. They can nearly
always claim, with some justification, that the goods and services

they produce for the domestic economy and/or for convertible-currency exports are essential. In the current precarious status of Hungary's balance of payments, a government threat to replace the production of delinquent enterprises with imports, or to do without their exports, is not taken seriously.

152   Politically, managers of large enterprises also represent a powerful lobby, forming a critical "interlocking directorate" with top ministry and other government and party officials, who, in effect, exercise many collective ownership functions. Together, they can always present the continued bailout of this or that enterprise as necessary to "the national interest."

153   Banks might be expected to discipline the delinquent enterprises, but they seldom if ever do so. Indeed, as regards involuntary, or psuedo-credit, banks themselves may engage in the same practices with other banks and their own suppliers. Also, banks often have only a few large enterprises as customers and are therefore hesitant to move against them. This is especially so, moreover, because the newly established banks have only small reserves.

154   Take a typical large commercial bank, any one of the five that control the flow of credit to much of the economy. When these banks were created in 1987, they were given an arbitrary portfolio of assets (loans to enterprises outstanding) and liabilities (the deposits of enterprises). A good number of their loans are not being "serviced" today. In a normal economy, the bank would have to "write off" bad loans or foreclose on the borrower, collecting what it could. If the bank had too many "non-performing" loans, it would have to go bankrupt. In Hungary, in any case, the government so far has not forced the banks to collect on the bad loans, or to write them off.

155   It is not surprising, then, that banks act on the basis of short-term motivation. So long as new loans can help maintain the illusion that the old loans are still good, there is pressure to provide new credit. The banks also have shirked any responsibility to withhold credit for payment of wages, and not only is there no law requiring them to prevent this practice, but until 1987 there was a "general

rule" to provide such credit. And since the banking structure is oligopolistic, the banks know that the government could not afford to see any one of them go bankrupt.

Thus, regardless of motivations, present behavior by those who are in charge of partly state-owned commercial banks and state-owned enterprises is not in conformity with the rational behavior of counterparts in well-functioning market economies.   **156**

These are the reasons that tight monetary policy alone will not be able to set the economy right and to control inflation. The improved effectiveness of monetary policy--and of money generally --is partly a function of fundamental changes in the economic system. Real owners must be developed through privatization. Financial discipline must be imposed on banks and on producers by strengthening import and domestic competition, by deconcentration of monopolies, and by introducing more prudent rules, regulations, and business practices.   **157**

The immediate policy goal should be to help create an economy in which money is the primary means for resource allocation at the micro-level and of economic control at the macro-level. At the present time money fulfills these functions poorly. Only significant progress in overcoming this deficiency will make it possible for the monetary authorities to serve a more traditional purpose, which is to help create a strong and stable currency by controlling inflation, consistent with restructuring of the economy and encouraging growth.   **158**

Achieving and monitoring a strong and stable currency should be the highest economic priority of the new economic management in the next three years. This will mean reducing the annual rate of inflation to a single digit (preferably to a low single digit). Achieving such an objective without impeding market forces would generate overwhelming domestic and international goodwill for the new government, would establish one of the main cornerstones of sustained prosperity, and would support immeasurably Hungary's case for admission to the European Community.   **159**

160   Hungary must have a limited central authority in the economy but
a strong one. One area where it surely must be strong is in
monetary policy. First, and foremost, the conduct of monetary
policy must be made more effective by creating or strengthening
the institutions, the instruments, the business practices, and the
policies that impose financial discipline on enterprises and banks
(i.e., "sanitize" the system of pseudo-credit). Second, the economy must "digest" the inflationary pressures that the new government inherited from the old regime, and it must do this without
allowing temporary inflation, which is inevitable, to accelerate
and become permanently high inflation. And third, the conduct of
monetary policy has to be insulated from short-term social and
political pressures.

161   It is especially important to provide a strong monetary authority
because it must deal with the inflationary pressures that the new
government has inherited, pressures that will be notably intense
during the first several years of the transition, owing to the following factors:

- Hungary's move to a convertible-currency settlement
  with CMEA countries will generate terms of trade and
  other losses that must be financed.

- Reduction of subsidies are exerting an upward pressure
  on prices.

- Depreciation of the real exchange rate generates pressures
  for inflation.

- Servicing the large domestic and foreign debt reduces the
  supply of goods and services available to the domestic
  economy.

- Expected increases in nominal wages are likely to exceed
  productivity owing, among other reasons, to the sub-
  stitution by money wages of subsidies on consumer goods
  and services and payments in kind, and the expected rise

in unemployment will require added budget expenditures.

- Inflationary expectations are increasing.

Recommendations on Monetary Policy

The BRC's three recommendations on how to strengthen financial   **162**
discipline on banks and firms was pointed out in detail in Chapter
2 (paragraph 83).

During the transition period Hungary must also have an incomes   **163**
policy for state-owned enterprises. The wage bill paid by state-
owned enterprises must be kept within certain bounds. If and
when wage discipline weakens so much that it threatens to undermine the government's anti-inflation policies, the controls on
wages will have to be tightened.

In those few areas of the economy where enterprises still have   **164**
significant powers to set monopoly prices, and in selected areas of
agriculture and food, certain temporary controls on pricing should
be maintained. As conditions of competition take effect, controls
of all kinds should be removed.

Policies considered unacceptable for moderating inflation include   **165**
price freezes, administrative wage determination, and measures
that counteract the development of entrepreneurship and structural changes.

Monetary authority has to be insulated from day-to-day political   **166**
pressures so as to be in a position to resist the government
temptation to spend money that it does not have. A law on public
finance should restrict the central bank in crediting the state
budget (see paragraph 175). Another law has to institutionalize
the central bank's increased independence.

Special effort will have to be taken to abolish the large liquidity   **167**
generated by the trade surplus Hungary has with CMEA coun-

tries, among other reasons, because it adds to liquidity and thus fuels inflation.

168   The temptation will be to deal with all these issues through mere monetary fine-tuning. Clearly, the adequate management of monetary policy will require balancing restriction with the need for adequate levels of liquidity. In the agreements now being concluded with the IMF, provisions should be included on some form of adjustment of credit ceilings in the event of liquidity problems. Otherwise, the hardening budget constraint, the enforcement of payment discipline, and the avoidance of further accumulation of domestic payment arrears will result in an abrupt contraction of domestic output. The trend of increasing velocity will be reversed and severe dislocations in production could occur, without appropriate adjustment in credit expansion. Progress in establishing efficiently functioning capital markets also assumes adequate levels of liquid financial resources.

169   As the demand for money by enterprises shows an improved pattern, a special program needs to be developed for the prevention of new enterprises arrears stemming from the tight liquidity. This program should combine the mutual settlement of enterprise claims through the efficient intermediation of commercial banks and an appropriate liquidity infusion from the central bank. Concurrently, economic and legal safeguards need to be established to prevent the renewed accumulation of arrears.

170   In an effort to strengthen financial discipline, an improved system of supervision for banks (based on strict sanctions) and the implementation of a program to improve the accounting and auditing systems of enterprises and banks is recommended. Non-performing claims of commercial banks need to be closely monitored and an appropriate write-off procedure established. The supervisory agency would have explicit responsibility for examining banks with a view to determining the solvency of each of the bank's debtors. The supervisory agency also should have the authority to impose reserves and write-off requirements on banks with respect to sub-standard credits. It should also have the authority to remove management in cases where the loan portfolio

does not meet legally established minimal standards. Special banking activities have to be initiated for the management of un-collectible loan receivables of deposit money banks, which resulted from central decisions in the previous mono-bank system.

The oligopolistic nature of the Hungarian banking system needs to   **171** be reduced in order to enhance the efficiency of financial interme-diation and to improve the responsiveness of financial institutions to the needs of their customers, thereby offering greater choice and better service at lower cost. Entry into banking should also be opened for private concerns and individuals, too. Some members suggested separating commercial and investment banking func-tions of deposit money banks.

Monetary policy can be conducted more flexibly only through   **172** market-oriented instruments. To achieve this, the share of open market operations in conducting monetary policy needs to be increased. Refinancing should be done on market terms as op-posed to the quota system now in place.

Stabilization and transformation thus appear to require several   **173** bundles of significant measures over a period of two-to-three years, not a "big bang" at the beginning of the period, as is being tried in Poland.

Fiscal Policy

The budget of the general government should be balanced. The   **174** size of the budget should be reduced by substantial cuts in spen-ding. The ratio of subsidies should be reduced from 13% in 1988 to 5% of GDP by 1992. This program needs to focus on three areas: consumer, housing, and enterprise subsidies. An acceleration of the reduction in these subsidies, which distort production and consumption decisions, is highly desirable.

The legitimate fiscal operation of the public sector needs to be   **175** regulated by a law on public finance, which establishes a transpar-ent system of central budgeting, local budgeting and extra-budgetary funds. The number of extra-budgetary funds needs to be reduced. Procedural clarification and transparency is needed in respect to the relationship between the "valuation impact" on the foreign debt (i.e. losses from the depreciation of the forint) and the interest rate burden of the domestic debt.

176 Hungary today has a high level of taxation. It includes a 53% payroll tax (43% paid by the employer and 10% paid by the employee), a 50% marginal income tax rate, a 40% corporate profits tax, a value-added tax of up to 25%, plus many additional specific excise taxes. One objective of fiscal policy should be to reduce significantly the marginal tax burden on both producers and consumers--based on a medium-term program--in order to spur savings and investment, which will help fuel economic recovery and increase overall state revenues.

177 In order to encourage capital formation, retained earnings should be taxed at significantly lower rates than distributed earnings. Special consideration should be given to the preferential taxation of savings and capital gains and the principles of modernized depreciation schemes. Further efforts need to be made to reduce distortions and inequalities, making the tax system conform more closely to international standards. Reductions in exemptions are highly desirable if they are combined with the reduction of rates and widening of the tax base. These changes should improve the stability of tax revenues.

178 The tax administration agency should develop uniform accounting standards and conventions designed to assure that taxable net profit of business entities is calculated fairly and consistently with generally accepted accounting principles. Reasonable certainty of detection and punishment of tax evaders is a critical element of creating confidence in the tax system and encouraging voluntary compliance. Moreover, enforcement in itself is a substantial source of revenue production. The government should enter into arrangements with major market economies to provide for the exchange of information on these matters.

A thorough revision of social policy and the social security system   **179**
is needed in an effort to achieve the placing of revenues and
expenditures on a sustainable basis, as indicated in Chapter 6.

Chapter 5

INTEGRATING HUNGARY INTO THE INTERNATIONAL ECONOMY

The Situation and Problems

180   Foreign economic relations, until now, have been shaped largely by political considerations. Trade pacts with CMEA partners precluded competition, and foreign trade initiatives by Hungarian enterprises, until recently, were constrained and directed by central authorities. In an autarkic system, imports were not used to compete with domestic production, but to cover shortages. Foreign loans, instead of creating new productive strength, were used to prop up a declining living standard and to finance investments, many of which were not soundly prepared. Foreign economic dealings, therefore, have not been the engine for growth in Hungary that they have been in Western Europe or in other market economies.

181   Given domestic political developments and the changed external environment vis-a-vis the CMEA countries, Hungary's current foreign trade and investment institutions, structures and policies are not sustainable. Furthermore, approaches are required to stop the accumulation and to improve the uses and servicing of international debt.

Domestic Aspects of Foreign Trade Strategy

Hungary's main objective in its foreign economic relations should   **182**
be the establishment, with all deliberate speed, of a liberal foreign
trading regime and an export-oriented economic development
strategy.

Hungary should pursue an export-oriented development strat-   **183**
egy: liberalizing imports; ensuring the adequacy of trade-financ-
ing institutions; developing market information services, marketing capabilities, and training programs to enhance competitiveness on international markets; and preventing overvaluation of its
real exchange rates vis-a-vis convertible currencies. All of these
policies should operate in conformity with the international rules
of the General Agreement on Trade and Tariffs (GATT). Export
subsidies should be retained only selectively and temporarily.

To pursue trade liberalization, Hungary should continue to abol-   **184**
ish quantitative import restrictions, initially converting some of
these institutions into temporary duties, but with the strict proviso
that the law enacting them should also provide for their early
elimination, with a specific timetable written into the legislation.
Import liberalization also must go hand-in-hand with reestablish-
ment of macroeconomic control and microeconomic discipline on
firms.

Convertibility

Concerning the exchange rate vis-a-vis convertible currencies,   **185**
Hungary today has a "fixed" exchange rate regime, with the forint
tied to a trade-weighted basket of convertible currencies. This
official exchange rate is periodically adjusted by administrative
decision. There also exists a grey-market rate which is considerably lower than the official one.

Hungary already has achieved significant partial convertibility: **186**
for foreigners, on certain transactions, including guaranteed repa-
triation of the principal invested as well as profit, plus all imports
by a joint venture or other foreign entities; and for domestic

businesses, on liberalized imports (about two-thirds of total imports).

187   There is full agreement in the BRC that an essential objective of the new government should be to attain the full convertibility of the forint for all transactions in the current and capital accounts, for domestic and foreign businesses and for residents alike. The forint should be tied to a strong West European currency or currency basket, at a fixed rate.

188   Full convertibility is highly desirable for several reasons. It would integrate Hungary's markets fully. It would give a wide range of purchase choices to its firms and consumers, and thereby promote exports and enhance consumer satisfaction, promote import competition, and make Hungary much more attractive to foreign investors. Currency speculation, a notoriously unattractive, demoralizing, and confidence-destroying aspect of economic life, would stop.

189   Tying the forint to a strong currency at a fixed rate also would represent a commitment by Hungary's new government to price stability (single-digit rate of inflation), thereby making Hungary that much more attractive to foreigners as a business partner and giving Hungarians themselves another incentive for entrepreneurship.

190   Achieving full convertibility at a sustainable fixed exchange rate also would be the best economic preparation that Hungary's new government could make to strengthen its case for membership in the European Community. Indeed, it is hard to imagine the EC giving serious consideration to Hungary's application until and unless convertibility is achieved.

191   As to when convertibility at a fixed rate can be reached, all in the BRC agree that essential preconditions are more effective monetary policy and the imposition of financial discipline on enterprises and banks.

There is disagreement within the BRC, however, as to sequencing   192
and timing. One group recommends that the forint should be
made convertible quickly, perhaps letting it float temporarily to let
the market determine its value without any government interference. The advocates of this approach stress the benefits of a
uniform foreign exchange rate and market (versus today's seg-
mented official and grey markets), the availability of uniform
international price signals, increased freedom, ease, and security
for individuals and firms to engage in international transactions,
and the real as well as symbolic importance of such a commitment
to the principles of a free market. Putting off convertibility very
long, they argue, merely postpones real economic recovery and
Hungary's development as a modern economy accepted into the
integrated world economy as a full partner.

Others, who consider such steps premature, stress that in the eco-   193
nomic and psychological environment in which Hungary finds
itself today and which it is likely to face tomorrow, letting the
forint float would lead to its quick depreciation, which is not
even fully justifiable economically. This would further strengthen
already dangerous inflationary pressures. At this early stage of
the transformation, they argue, monetary policy cannot become
sufficiently effective to control inflation. Therefore, they recommend a more gradual approach, concentrating concurrently on institutional reform, achieving financial discipline in the micro-
sphere, holding down inflation, and setting such an exchange
rate that would allow a substantial share of exports (practically
all industrial goods and services) to be profitable without reliance
on special subsidies. Convertibility would be increased in steps
by further import liberalization and the removal of controls on
additional cross-border transactions.

Whichever path is selected, the new government should discuss   194
the matter early, and then set a course and announce it, so that all
elements in society can anticipate the changes and begin to adjust
to them. All on the BRC also agree that the new government
should target the full convertibility of the forint at a fixed rate
within approximately three years.

External Aspects of Foreign Trade Strategy

195 Hungary should seek full membership in the European Community. Pending attainment of full membership, it should seek an associate status that would bring it the freest possible access to the European Common Market, as well as the earliest possible conformity of Hungary's product and process standards with those of the EC.

196 Following up on its October 1989 official proposal, Hungary should try to conclude, within three to five years, a free trade agreement with each EFTA country, phasing out quantitative restrictions and eliminating customs duties.

197 Opening up or significant marketization of Hungary's economy would be impossible without fundamental reforms in the country's trade relations vis-a-vis CMEA partners. The essence of the necessary and inevitable reforms is discontinuation of existing state trading practices, placing relations with CMEA partners on a commercial market basis, and switching from the present transferable ruble (TR) system to one based on convertible currencies. To help finance the trade that Hungary's profit-seeking enterprises will want to conduct, new institutional arrangements will be required. Western commercial banks may be in a position to assist. The need for such reforms is underscored by the crisis in the economies of the USSR and Eastern Europe and in intra-CMEA trade relations.

198 The most important benefit of the switch to dollar payments would be that Hungarian enterprise managers would encounter a more unified external economic environment, prompting them to make sounder business decisions. New pressures would be placed on Hungarian firms to improve the efficiency and quality of their exports to all destinations because the sheltered nature of the Eastern market would cease to exist and firms no longer would be able to rely on the crutch of state subsidies for fulfilling foreign trade obligations entered into by their own authorities.

These welcome changes, however, will involve large, if tempo-   **199**
rary, micro- and macro-economic costs. The combined impacts of
price, structure, and volume changes in trade with the CMEA,
principally with the USSR, are likely to be a sharp deterioration in
Hungary's balance of convertible trade, estimated to be in the
range of $1.0 billion to $1.5 billion in the first year of the transition.
This imbalance, fortunately, is expected to decline continually as
adjustments take place in production, exports, and imports.

Hungary should strive to build new forms of cooperation with its   **200**
reform-oriented neighbors in Eastern Europe, such as creating a
free trade area, with a view toward mutually strengthening each
others' outward-looking policies and integration into the world
economy.

Foreign Direct Investment (FDI)

Today no country in the world can afford the luxury of relying   **201**
only on its own resources to increase productivity and competitiveness as well as the standard of living. FDI can contribute
significantly to the transformation and future development of
Hungary's economy. It will be insufficient for the full amount of
Hungary's needs for foreign capital, but it can meet a part of those
needs. The current proportion of foreign ownership in many small
West European countries is about one-third of the country's
industry. At the beginning of 1990, foreigners own only about 2%
of Hungary's industry, so by any reasonable standard there is
ample room for expansion.

FDI provides a range of benefits through the generation of addi-   **202**
tional economic activities and employment: the development of
entrepreneurship, the transfer and diffusion of technology and
management know-how, and improved penetration of foreign
markets. In Hungary's case, FDI particularly will assist in the
restructuring of noncompetitive enterprises with capital, technology and greater export orientation. However, the extent and
nature of the benefits flowing from foreign investment are a
function of both the host country's policies concerning foreign

investors and the responses of investors to those policies. Very important is the degree and character of the integration of FDI within the local economy. The greater the integration and linkage, the larger the benefits. In general, the conditions that will attract FDI to Hungary are the same as the conditions that provide for healthy development of the domestic sector.

- Foreign investors should be treated the same as local investors. The corporate income tax system should be re-examined (1) to determine the wisdom of granting foreign joint ventures across-the-board tax advantages that are not available to domestic investors, and (2) to assure, as soon as the overall status of the fiscal balance allows, that the overall and marginal tax rate is not excessive.

- Hungary's evolving financial markets should be opened for direct access by foreign investors, for the purpose of conducting their activities in Hungary.

- Screening and approval procedures for FDI should be predictable, transparent, and minimal. This does not preclude controls and restrictions on FDI in certain sectors if Hungary's policy-makers, after thorough analysis and evaluation, find this appropriate. However changes to laws affecting foreign investment should be kept to a minimum. Frequent changes and contradictory signals from new laws and institutions create an uncertain investment climate and constrict the inflow of investment.

203 Developing an investment promotion program that highlights Hungary's advantages is a challenge that the new government will have to meet. Competition for international investment is keen now, and worldwide. While there are many organizations in Hungary that promote the inflow of foreign investment, they are not yet as skilled and assertive as their counterparts in North America and Western Europe. Hungary's investment promotion efforts should be orchestrated by a new "Invest Hungary" agency, similar to those trade agencies found in many localities around the world. This agency should be able to provide the information that investors need and to increase the ability to mount "investment prospecting programs" directed to specific investors.

International Financial Cooperation

Implementation of the Action Program outlined in this report will   **204**
lead to sustained improvements in the Hungarian economy's productivity, export competitiveness, external creditworthiness, and the standard of living, making it possible for Hungary gradually to achieve the same general level of economic activity as is found in the rest of Western Europe.

If the Action Program is successful during the next three years   **205**
(1991-1993), Hungary's imports will increase at a rapid pace. This is not bad news but good news. The causes will be the decisive further liberalization of imports and the significant inflow of FDI, which will be accompanied by additional investments in modernization and capacity expansion, as well as production for the domestic market and for export.

Although Hungary will pursue a long-term export-oriented   **206**
development strategy, there will be a lag between the inflow of FDI and imports and the resulting increase in exports. This lag, along with the huge restructuring of the nation's CMEA trade, will mean that during these coming three years Hungary should not be expected to run an export surplus on its combined trade and services account.

Also, Hungary owes more than $20 billion to foreign creditors. Re-   **207**
grettably, this money was not used for sound investments that could generate the foreign exchange earnings to service the debt. Thus, even with the principal rolled over, Hungary has to obtain additional capital imports of about $1 billion to $1.5 billion per year for each of the next three years in order to turn a potentially large net outflow into a small net inflow.

As noted before, Hungary will engage in an aggressive policy of   **208**
seeking foreign direct investment. Part of the capital inflow should

be used to reduce Hungary's external debt. The remaining part of the financing gap can be covered by obtaining the kind of assistance from governments and other organizations that will not add to Hungary's debt-service burden.

209   The commitment that Hungary's previous government made to the IMF for 1990--namely, to generate a surplus of about $1 billion on the combined trade and services account--should be adhered to. Beyond agreements already in effect, Hungary should initiate negotiations with international financial institutions on new facilities. The BRC believes that the desired levels of FDI and financial assistance for 1991-1993 cannot be expected to materialize unless and until Hungary's new government implements a program that will instill confidence in the international community, demonstrating that the prospects for Hungary's economy are bright and that the government will improve the precarious creditworthiness that it inherited. This can be achieved only through a strong commitment by Hungary's new government to the kind of Action Program sketched out in this report.

210   If, however, international lenders believe that new loans would simply be used, for example, to shore up living standards, then added substantial new assistance probably will not be offered.

211   It will be very difficult for Hungary's new government to take the steps necessary for laying the foundations of its sustained recovery and transformation (i.e., simultaneous stabilization and liberalization) unless it has some assurance that it can count on international financial cooperation during the difficult transition period of approximately three years. The new government of Hungary should note, therefore, that the IMF can provide "catalytic support" to member countries. An agreement on economic policies between the Fund and a member country often catalyzes financing from other sources because it gives governments, financial institutions, and investors some confidence that the country is adopting policies and reforms that address its fundamental economic problems.

The BRC is of the opinion that it would be tragic if a lack of under-   212
standing and response from the international community were to
undermine the chances of success of Hungary's speedy transition
to a market economy and stable political democracy.

Any temporary financial assistance that governments, interna-   213
tional organizations, and private groups would grant to Hungary
should be dedicated to help finance:

- the foreign exchange cost of import liberalization;

- the foreign exchange cost of switching from transferable
  ruble to dollar accounting in CMEA trade; and

- the cost of investment for environmental protection.

One significant and politically feasible form of help would be   214
Western governments' guarantees for commercial loans made to
Hungary, since such guarantees would ease the flow and lower
the risk, and thus the cost, of such credits. Western governments
also should offer tax concessions to their nationals and corpora-
tions investing in Hungary and elsewhere in Eastern Europe.

The BRC recommends that Hungary should pledge that a signifi-   215
cant share of the foreign exchange proceeds of privatization
would be set aside to reduce its foreign debt.

Western Assistance

In addition to the financial assistance sketched above: 216

- In commercial policy, the substantial easing of Western
  import restrictions is a sine qua non of Hungary's own
  speedy trade liberalization.

- There is little further justification to maintain present
  COCOM restrictions on Western technology exports that
  Hungary needs for its domestic economy.

- Hungary should be granted the same trade preferences, including GSP, that countries around the world comparable to Hungary receive from the developed market economies.

217 Hungary's transformation process would benefit from bilateral and multilateral technical assistance in a range of fields including tax administration, the statistical system, public administration, entrepreneurial training, foreign investment laws and promotion, labor laws, retraining, and help in creation of an expanded sector of voluntary associations.

Chapter 6

SOCIAL POLICY

Legacies

218   The social policies of communism in Hungary both failed the needy citizenry and damaged the economy. Social programs were constructed under the old system with the assumption that certain problems, such as unemployment, simply would not arise. It also was assumed that taking care of other social needs would be fully the responsibility of the state. The resulting social programs finally imagined that the central authorities would know best the needs of each individual, and that it was not necessary to take into account individual personal motives and incentives or the desire to be self-reliant. The universal social programs built on these assumptions turned out to be dysfunctional and so costly as to be unsustainable in the budget. In practice, even the education and health systems became monopolies of the state. Social systems such as market-conforming labor relations and unemployment compensation are undeveloped. The new government will find that social policy systems must also be reorganized and redirected. The Blue Ribbon Commission cannot focus on the whole social issues field, but does examine how certain social programs effect the economy.

219   Hungary's social expenditures are reflected in the following data:

- Housing subsidies alone consume 15% of the central budget. Much of this goes to middle- and higher-income individuals.

- Subsidies on other items, including, food, water, transportation, and agriculture, consume another 13% of the central budget.

- Retirement and health care expenditures are financed by a social security fund that is balanced by a payroll tax amounting to 53% of salary, a percent that is significantly higher than in Western Europe.

- The retirement system not only is costly but places Hungary at a substantial economic disadvantage relative to other nations. The retirement age is 55 for women and 60 for men. In most Western European nations, it is 65 for both. Retirement benefits in Hungary are based on the wages paid by the employer over the last three years of employment, rather than largely on contributions made by the employee, as is the case in most developed nations.

The Blue Ribbon Commission fully understands the political sen-   **220**
sitivity of each of these programs, inasmuch as they fundamen-
tally affect the life of every family. Nevertheless, the present social
system cannot be sustained as is; it must be changed to reduce the
costs of compulsory programs, to provide wider choice for the
citizens, and to improve the efficiency of service delivery.

The Commission strongly recommends that the new government   **221**
immediately draft detailed policies to achieve a new, more hu-
mane and cost-effective social system. In the meantime, the BRC
offers some conceptual ideas that would channel the changes in a
positive direction.

Health Care

International figures show that during the past two decades the   **222**
health status of the Hungarian population actually has deterio-
rated and the overall level of general health care is extremely low
compared to other countries. To improve the situation, new
emphasis should be placed on prevention (e.g. education and

publicity about the dangers of smoking and poor diet; screening for cancer and blood and heart diseases). Such public health measures can produce notable improvements in a relatively few years.

223 Today, practically all health care is financed from central resources, which are limited; and the money is spent inefficiently. Under-the-table payment for medical services has become a widely practiced phenomenon, which is degrading and permits tax evasion. Many doctors and patients alike are demoralized.

224 A general reform of the health care system is obviously necessary, but the existing health care system has to function while the transition is taking place.

225 A universal health service should be established with wide coverage and compulsory contributions by employees. Its funding should be administered separately from old age pensions and other social services in order to clarify where and how funds are being spent.

226 The institutional arrangements in the national health insurance system should provide incentives for health-care personnel to provide high quality service, at prices affordable for the citizens who pay for it in taxes. The system should operate fairly and be transparent enough that it is easily perceived as fair. One option for a new system that meets the above criteria and has proven to work well in other countries would be the following:

- The private practice of medicine, including the operation of private medical facilities, should be called to life, on a non-discriminating basis. Each Hungarian citizen should have the right to choose freely his or her doctor and medical institution, irrespective of who owns the facility or where the citizen resides.

- A central health insurance board should publish and revise periodically a "health service price list," enumerating cost-based prices for medical services.

- The Ministry of Health should establish professional and technical standards for all providers of medical services. Personnel meeting those standards should be automatically licensed and authorized to invoice the health insurance board for services rendered, in accordance with the price list. Any violation of the professional standards, or fraud, would cause the institution or individual to be excluded from participation in the basic service financing.

- Concurrently with introduction of such a system, general state budgetary support for the providers of medical services should be discontinued.

- Each Hungarian employee should continue to be required to make regular health insurance contributions in exchange for coverage under the compulsory basic health insurance. The amount of contribution should be in proportion to income, up to a certain limit. The basic level of health care would be guaranteed to every citizen of Hungary.

- Extra services should be financed by the patient directly or via his voluntary participation in a profit-oriented private insurance system.

The BRC is divided on the issue of whether full-cost coverage for   **227** the patient should be reserved for major medical (including catastrophic) illnesses or for all medical services. The majority of the BRC believes that the costs of routine medical services and related prescription drugs should be reimbursed only in part except, on a means-tested basis, for patients with very low income. Personal contributions by patients are widely considered to be a disincentive for casual over-use of the health care system, thereby unfairly raising costs for the system and the taxes that support it.

Education

228   A hallmark of policy concerning education should be a decisive move away from the near-monopoly exercised by the state in this domain. Private education encourages competition for students, which in turn spurs greater efforts by public and private institutions alike. A variety of educational forms also encourages innovation in teaching methods and other improvements. Rapid progress is needed toward decentralization of authority over state-sponsored schools to local administration. Within the latter, a strong parental role in overseeing education is also to be sought through locally elected school boards.

229   In higher education, the admission system should be changed. More persons should be given the opportunity to enter by using more comprehensive criteria for admission. Thereafter, only those who perform well at acceptable levels should be retained. The overall result will be an expansion in the number of university graduates, a boon to the economic life and social progress of the Republic.

230   The method of financing higher education should be changed. In addition to scholarships, students should be expected to pay for at least a part of their education, either concurrently through savings or part-time employment, or on a deferred basis through loans. If students bear some of the cost of their education in these ways, state funding for universities can be improved.

Housing

231   Housing represents a huge and unsustainable drain on the state budget, causes serious distortions in the effectiveness of fiscal and monetary policies, and involves huge subsidies whose distribution is socially unjust.

232   The construction of private flats and houses currently is subsidized in different ways. A lump sum allowance is provided for young couples with children. Until 1988, preferential, fixed-

rate housing loans (3% for 35 years) were available; the subsidized servicing of these loans is slated to continue for several decades.

Housing expenditures in the budget (including the interest rate   **233**
subsidy) have grown in recent years: in 1989, 15% of the budget
outlays were allocated for housing finance. Distortions are inten-
sified by the fact that two-thirds of subsidies go to those already
occupying a flat, irrespective of their income position.

A radical modernization of housing finance is a must. The state has   **234**
an indispensable role in eliminating present tensions and distortions, creating a more equitable distribution of the burden of
housing expenses, reducing budgetary expenditures for housing,
and maintaining the housing stock more effectively. The burden
on households will increase considerably during the economic
transformation. The state should cover part of the costs for families in difficult income situations, with the amount established by
a means test.

The present apartment-rental system should be changed, over a   **235**
five-year period, to market-based leasing.

The entire sector of state-owned apartments should become glob-   **236**
ally self-financing in three years. The rent of each apartment
should be adjusted to reflect its real condition (based on location,
size, and quality). Free-market rents should be allowed to emerge
for state-owned apartments of the best quality.

Urban housing renewal, neglected in the past, should be financed   **237**
from other sources.

The current process of privatizing state-owned flats should con-   **238**
tinue. A procedure should be established to move selling prices
closer to real market values.

Changing the terms of the outstanding mortgage debts stipulated   **239**
in the old credit agreements is inevitable. The purpose is to
discontinue (1) the unreasonable windfall gains to the debtors

resulting from the substantial inflation after the contracts were entered into and (2) the corresponding huge losses incurred by the state budget. The revision can be implemented in alternative ways, including indexing the debts to inflation, adding the interest subsidy to personal income, and taxing this gain at the personal-income tax rate of each borrower, or adding a significant upward adjustment in each borrower's debt-service obligation to reflect past inflation.

240   It is absolutely necessary for the government not to enter into any more mortgage contracts which involve interest subsidies. New mortgage contracts should be provided by free credit markets. In general, subsidies should be given to people because they are poor and not because they occupy particular dwellings. But if, per contra, subsidies are attached to housing of the poor, then the subsidies should be independent of, and not distort, capital markets. They should also be quite transparent--such as up-front cash subsidies.

241   Concurrently with the above adjustment, the increased cost of rents and maintenance will have to be reflected in wages and pensions.

242   The government should find ways to assist increasing the housing stock, especially in cities. On the one hand, this requires that instead of the huge, inefficient monopoly real-estate-managing organizations, small, independent, and flexible housing units should be created under free-market conditions. At the same time, it would be desirable to help local governments find ways to assist the development of private housing in order to improve the supply of housing. This would also help dampen the speculative fever in real estate, which is contributing to housing prices that have become unaffordable for most young persons.

243   The government should announce and discuss as soon as possible its intention to make these changes, thus enabling groups in society with different interests to start adjusting to the inevitable new conditions during the next several years.

All subsidies for basic services (such as water and energy) should   **244**
be phased out within three years.

The implementation of the BRC's recommendations concerning   **245**
the housing program is one of the central issues of the entire
Action Program, owing to its substantial financial, moral, and
social impacts. Maintenance of the existing system would prevent
a fundamental change between the scope of the state and the
market, hinder the lowering of taxes, and undermine economic
stabilization. Confidence in the new government would be im-
paired significantly if the prevailing unjust system of burden-shar-
ing in this area were to remain unchanged.

Social Security Programs

Retirement Pensions

Presently, retirement pensions for men from 60 years of age and   **246**
women 55 years of age are paid as a fraction of the average of the
last three years of salary or wage. This rule distorts wage arrangements since there is a great incentive to both employer and
employee to trade lower wages until the age of 57 (for men) or 52
(for women) against massive increases over the last three years.
This then maximizes the pensioner's claim on the state. A more
fundamental problem is that the state pension received does not
depend on contributions and the rate of return on those contributions, but on the open-ended commitments between employees
and employers and the state's ability and willingness to raise tax
revenue and print money to cover those commitments.

Present Hungarian policy concerning the age of retirement reflects   **247**
poorly the emerging demographic reality of an age distribution
characterized by a high ratio of the retired to the working-age
population. The institutionalized difference between female and
male ages of retirement is also anomalous and discriminatory.
Early consideration should be given to the gradual raising of the
age of retirement and to the abolition of the distinction between
male and female ages of retirement. (Earlier retirement should

remain an option, but it should entail a penalty in terms of reduced pension benefits.)

248 Preservation of the real purchasing power of social security-provided pensions and adjustment of such pensions should be declared goals of social policy. But such adjustment should remain subject to explicit consideration of the merit of the case.

249 In the medium term, Hungary should consider switching to a pension system fully funded by private contributions. [Different views were expressed on whether a part and what part of these private contributions should be compulsory.] This would insulate the budget from pension demands and, conversely, remove the temptation of funding other government expenditures through the pension fund. Furthermore, permitting competitive pension funds will provide a nucleus for a capital market and an incentive for the worker to seek out a high performance fund to which to entrust his pension contributions. This would provide incentive to funds to perform most productively in the interest of the pensioner, and at the same time promote personal responsibility on the part of the pension-seeker.

250 It is essential to separate clearly the pension system from the welfare system. The pension payment should depend on contributions, while welfare benefits should depend on other criteria. Much more latitude can be given for private supplemental ("topping up") pensions and for switching to different forms of benefit streams.

251 The transition from a distorted retirement system to a privately funded system can be established in five years.

Social Safety Net

252 The social safety net should rest on two pillars: unemployment compensation and assistance to the needy.

253 Improving efficiency in most industries and services will result in the release of labor, often in a geographically highly concentrated fashion. The anticipated initial rise of open unemployment and the long-term prospect of a substantial frictional unemployment necessitate the introduction of a relief scheme as a crucial element of the government's social safety net.

In the longer run, unemployment should be handled as a statistical   **254**
risk. An unemployment insurance fund should be set up, financed from a separately identified payroll tax. Compensation paid from this fund would be due to unemployed persons (i.e., persons actively seeking work) with a previous employment record. The level of such compensation would be related to previous earnings but would be subject to a cap. It would have to be appreciably below the relevant wage level, in order to discourage opportunistic use, and it would have to be limited to a flexibly set, finite period of job search. In a starting period--if necessary--the unemployment insurance fund will have to be appropriately fed and replenished from general revenue sources. The problem of involuntary total employee disability would be handled as an integral part of social security insurance.

A substantial fraction of the unemployment that will emerge   **255**
during transformation is likely to be of structural character, i.e. representing a situation of mismatch between the skills of job-seekers and the skills that the expanding market economy demands. Programs organized to retrain workers in new skills can make an important contribution to mitigating this problem, as outlined in Chapter 3.

A negative income tax, together with a simple progressive tax at   **256**
higher income levels, may be considered because (1) it provides assistance to the needy, (2) it retains an incentive for the unemployed and those who earn low wages to search for (better) work, and (3) it can be combined with the personal income tax system.

Chapter 7

PROGRAM OF THE
FIRST 100 DAYS

257   Hungary's economy cannot wait. For economic as well as political reasons, the new government should move quickly and decisively to present a comprehensive economic program. The program should establish priorities and be as concrete and time-specific as possible. The main actions which the BRC believes the new government should take during its first 100 days, in accordance with the overall Action Program we propose, are summarized as follows.

258   In privatization and promoting entrepreneurship:

- Undertake specific measures to promote private entrepreneurship (paragraph 59).

- Express regret to those who suffered after 1947 under nationalization without appropriate compensation, and assist any of those who are still in dire need as a result of nationalization.

- Under stated guidelines, initiate privatization of a significant number of enterprises; enact a law on privatization (and include employee ownership options), and modify the Enterprise Law, the Law on Land, and the Law on Cooperatives.

- Establish new strategic guidelines and an investment agency, "Invest Hungary," to attract foreign capital to certain crucial and under-financed sectors, such as tele-communications.

In building the institutional framework for the market: **259**

- Pass a law on competition policy (paragraphs 107-112).

- Continue deconcentration and deregulation, and abolish the administrative rules on setting interest rates.

- Improve the Bankruptcy Law and assure enforcement.

- Convert import restrictions into temporary tariffs and then concurrently announce a firm timetable for the re-duction of such tariffs (paragraph 184).

In creating macro-economic stability, social policy and govern-   **260**
ment activities:

- Maintain tight monetary and fiscal policies.

- Announce and implement the fiscal measures necessary to achieve the subsidy- and deficit-reduction targets (paragraph 174).

- Announce the government's time-specific commitment to convertibility at a fixed exchange rate, with the forint tied to a stable European currency (paragraph 194).

- Move the exchange rate closer to that recommended in the Action Program (paragraphs 187-193).

- Impose strong financial discipline on state enterprises; initiate bankruptcy proceeding against enterprises with tax and other payments in arrears to the government (paragraph 83).

- Announce an agriculture policy that emphasizes export efficiency and the reorientation of farming from giant enterprises to private farms, based on efficiency criteria (paragraphs 136-138).

- Pass new laws on central and commercial banking (paragraphs 166, 170, 171).

- Take the administrative steps necessary to achieve the ruble-foreign-trade targets for 1990.

- Pass laws to transform tax policy, including local tax and spending authority (paragraphs 175-178).

- Create an appropriate social safety net; clarify the status of workers and employees; and liberalize the laws related to employment and labor contracts (paragraphs 252-255).

- Announce the principles, the tasks, and an implementation program on housing (paragraphs 234-244).

- Undertake public hearings to explain the government's plans and to hear citizens' concerns firsthand.

261 Urgent international initiatives:

- Take a concerted set of actions to assure that the economy will have a net capital inflow during 1991-93 (paragraphs 208-209).

- Initiate steps to seek associate membership in the European Community (paragraph 195).

- Begin negotiations on free trade agreements with individual EFTA countries (paragraph 196).

- Revise the system of intra-CMEA financial cooperation in trade and on regulations that affect tourism.

- Initiate regional coordination of environmental policies (paragraph 142).

- Request bilateral and multilateral technical assistance in a range of fields (paragraph 217).

Each item in the above list should represent either a concrete step   **262**
on the part of the government or a firm and irrevocable commitment by it that it will take the steps necessary to implement the
policies announced.

APPENDIX

Appendix A:
Acknowledgments

On behalf of our fellow members of the Blue Ribbon Commission, we must thank the individuals and organizations in Hungary and elsewhere who brought us together and supported our work.

The Blue Ribbon Commission was convened by three Hungarian and four international organizations. In Hungary, they are: the Hungarian Academy of Sciences, the Hungarian Chamber of Commerce, and the Budapest University of Economic Sciences. These organizations established the Blue Ribbon Foundation to support this function. Abroad, they are: the East-West Forum, Indiana University, Hudson Institute, and the Nomura Research Institute. Additional details on these seven organizations are found in Appendix B. The BRC extends its profound thanks to these organizations and their executives.

Major additional financial, institutional, and technical support was received in Hungary from Rolitron Bioeletronics, Ltd., the National Planning Office, Novotrade, the Budapest Local Transport Company, and the National Technological Development Committee. Support abroad was provided by The Pew Charitable Trusts, the U.S. National Council for Soviet and East European Research, the Ford Foundation, E.I. du Pont de Nemours and Company, Eli Lilly and Company, the Lilly Endowment, Inc., Dow Chemical Europe, Proctor and Gamble, Inc., Guardian Industries, Dr. Beurt SerVaas, SerVaas Incorporated, the Cummins Engine Foundation, the Central Soya Corporation, and the Arvin Foundation, Inc.

Truly indispensable to the work of BRC has been the limitless dedication and monumental work of the co-managing directors of the project and the Foundation: Dr. István Hetényi, Professor of Economics at the University of Economic Sciences (Budapest), and a former Minister of Finance, and Dr. Paul Marer, Professor of International Business at Indiana University (Bloomington). These two men organized and coordinated the efforts of the working groups, prepared the initial drafts, and edited the final drafts. The inexhaustible Dr. Marer was in many ways the "guiding light" of the project. He personifies the bridge in the BRC logo--the essential link with each other person and with all activities of the BRC Project.

In Budapest, Dr. Csaba Gelényi has served as coordinator of the project in Hungary, handling with dedication a myriad of administrative matters and volunteering his time on many evenings and weekends. Diana Kósa and Katalin Márer organized several support activities relating to the BRC's work, especially in connection with the Budapest meeting. László Antal contributed organizationally as well as intellectually. László Rózsahegyi of Rolitron, Arpad Abonyi of Prospectus, Inc. (Canada) and Gyula Tellér generously guided the layout and publication of the final document, in Hungarian and in English. György Varga ably managed a number of publicity tasks.

A key role was played by Indiana University doctoral candidate and Hudson Research Analyst Erik Whitlock, who spent six months in Budapest helping to prepare the drafts and serving as liaison between the Hungarian and international teams. Also indispensable to the Commission's work were the efforts of Hudson Research Analyst and Program Coordinator Amy Beth Hutchison, who coordinated innumerable logistical and other details connected with the BRC's four meetings, often volunteering evenings and weekends.

Hudson Institute played a pivotal role in this project. It coordinated and hosted the BRC's first meeting. More than one hundred specialists from fifteen countries attended and worked at the week-long meeting at Hudson's headquarters in Indianapolis,

Indiana, in January 1990. Hudson also coordinated the BRC's second and third meetings in Brussels and Vienna in February. More than a dozen Hudson professionals contributed to BRC working groups. Hudson served as the international secretariat of the Commission and participated in crafting the final version of the BRC's report in English. Particularly significant Hudson contributions came from Richard W. Judy, Director of the Center for Soviet and Central European Studies, who initiated and directed Hudson's overall role in the BRC and substantially contributed to each phase of its work; Mitchell E. Daniels, Jr., President, who consistently supported Hudson's involvement in the project; Ambassador Bruce Chapman, as a senior advisor to the project who also assisted in drafting the final report in Budapest; and Stuart Methven, who went out of his way to organize the meetings of the BRC in Brussels.

East-West Forum and its Executive Director, James Montgomery, were dedicated and especially helpful in getting this project off the ground and in arranging financial support, working closely with George Kendall of Economic Strategies and Carol Connell of the Seagram Corporation.

Indiana University and its President, Thomas Ehrlich, hosted the BRC, as did the School of Business with its Dean, Jack Wenworth. The Indiana Center for Global Business coordinated Indiana University's involvement in the project, under Directors Lawrence Davidson and Pat Eoyang. A dozen Indiana University professors made intellectual contributions to the project.

The BRC wishes to acknowledge the cooperation of experts from international organizations--the World Bank, the International Monetary Fund (IMF), the United Nations Industrial Development Organization (UNIDO), and the European Community (EC). Their experts have exchanged views with members of the BRC and its working groups, in some cases participating in meetings. Similarly, there was an exchange of views in Washington, D.C., between several experts of the IMF and the World Bank and a group representing the BRC. All of these exchanges took place among individuals as experts and not as representatives of the organizations with which they are affiliated. The EC and UNIDO generously hosted BRC meetings in Brussels and Vienna, respectively.

Richard Rahn and David Burton of the United States Chamber of Commerce provided valuable analyses and critiques of the drafts, as did Dr. Lawrence Brainard of Bankers Trust Company, Walter van Daele of Putnam, Hayes and Bartlett, Peter Rona of IBJ Schroeder, Arpad Abonyi of Prospectus Incorporated, David Ellerman of Employee Ownership Services Inc., and Oliver Letwin of N. M. Rothschild. Geza Bankuty, founder and president of New England Machinery and co-chairman of the U.S.-Hungarian Economic Council, has contributed to the project from its inception and in many ways. The writings of Roger Douglas, New Zealand's former Minister of Finance, have inspired us on some of the proven approaches to managing the politics of economic transition.

The BRC's working groups labored long and hard to mobilize ideas and materials to support this report. Those groups and their co-chairs were:

> **Working Group I**, on privatization: Márton Tardos (co-chair of the BRC); János Martonyi (Head of the Governmental Task Force on Privatization, Budapest); Robert Campbell (Indiana University); and Ales Vahcic (University of Ljubljana).

> **Working Group II**, on establishing markets: Ferenc Vissi (Price Office, Budapest); Peter Lauter (George Washington University); and Roland Schönfeld (Sudosteuropa Gesellschaft, Munich).

> **Working Group III**, on integrating Hungary into the world economy: Andras Köves and Gábor Obláth (both at the Institute of Market Research, Budapest); Richard Judy (Hudson Institute); and György von O'sváth (Commission of the European Communities).

Working Group IV, on creating macro-economic stability: András Vértes (Economic Research Institute, Budapest); Richard Quandt (Princeton University); and Marie-Josee Drouin (Hudson Institute - Canada).

Working Group V, on social policy: Elemér Hankiss (Institute of Sociology, Budapest) and Paul Demeny (Population Council, New York).

Working Group VI, on the first 100 days' program: Kálmán Mizsei (Institute of World Economics, Budapest); Bela Balassa (John Hopkins University and the World Bank); and Pal Tar (Banque Nationale de Paris, France).

Sustained contributions that cut across several working groups also were made among others by: István Ábel, Mathew Ashe, Ákos Balassa, Joseph Battat, John Becker, Joel Bergsman, Richard Blue, Péter Ákos Bod, John Boquist, Joseph Brada, Keith Crane, Lawrence Davidson, Éva Ehrlich, John Erikson, Maurice Ernst, László Fodor, Janos Horvath, Michael Keeling, George Kendall, János Köllö, Iván Major, Seiichi Masuyama, Paul McCracken, Tsuneo Morita, Zoltan Pazmany, Kevin Quigley, Gábor Révész, Bella Rónaszéky, Beurt SerVaas, Roger Sperry, Nicholas Spulber, Istvan Telegdy, Hans and Sally Thorelli, András Timár, Joseph Tropea, Balint Vazsonyi, Edwin Wesely, William J. Williams, and Aladar Zichy.

Unfortunately, space does not allow us to thank individually the over 100 other persons who participated at various meetings in Indianapolis, Brussels, Vienna, and Budapest or contributed ideas and comments. Their contributions, too, were substantial and we trust that this final report reflects them.

Márton Tardos	**Sylvia Ostry**
Co-chair	Co-chair
Blue Ribbon Commission	Blue Ribbon Commission

Appendix B:
Sponsoring Organizations

The *Hungarian Academy of Sciences* is the supreme governing body of Hungary's scientific life. Established in 1825, the Academy has 36 research institutes with 8,500 employees (21 institutes in the natural and technical sciences and 15 in the social sciences and humanities). The ordinary, corresponding, and honorary members of the Academy are elected by secret ballot of the General Assembly of the Academy. Corresponding members are chosen from among those Ph.D.'s whose research results are judged outstanding by international standards. Members are selected from among the corresponding members. Honorary members are chosen from among foreign scholars whose work is especially appreciated by their Hungarian peers. The Academy's President is elected by the General Assembly. Professor Ivan Berend, who is a member of the Blue Ribbon Commission, is the current President.

The *Hungarian Chamber of Commerce* is the "citadel" of trade promotion in Hungary. Its role has evolved with the changes in economic management in Hungary. Before 1968, its tasks were restricted to the promotion of international economic relations, and only foreign trading companies were admitted as members. A presidential decree has institutionalized the Chamber's involvement in decisions on economic management. According to the decree, the Chamber is a social organization entrusted with the mediation, conciliation and representation of economic interests and is also called on to promote international economic relations. It is materially and organizationally independent from the state, and financed by the fees of the member enterprises. Nationwide this voluntary organization has more than 1800 members. The Chamber is an important forum for the exchange of opinions on Hungarian economic life. It is managed by a Presidium as well as by a managing Board elected by the members. László Fodor, Vice President of the Chamber, participated actively in the work of the Blue Ribbon Commission.

The *Budapest University of Economic Sciences* is Hungary's premier institution of higher education in the field of economics and the social sciences, with many outstanding faculty and students. Last year the university established a new School of Management with a curriculum designed to train the kinds of professionals who will be needed more and more as Hungary moves toward a market economy. The fact that during his July, 1989 visit to Hungary, President Bush delivered one of his major speeches at the University is symbolic of the forward-looking role that the University is playing within Hungary and in East-West relations. The current Rector of the University, Professor Csaba Csaki, is a member of the Blue Ribbon Commission.

Hudson Institute is a private, not-for-profit policy research organization that specializes in the study of policy problems and options for the public and private sectors. Hudson analysts take a creative and innovative approach to research, while stressing the importance of providing decision-makers with practical, usable analyses. It has headquarters in Indianapolis, Indiana, and offices in Washington, D.C.; Montreal, Canada; and Brussels, Belgium. Hudson Institute was founded in 1961 by the late Herman Kahn and colleagues from the Rand Corporation. The President of Hudson Institute is Mitchell E. Daniels, Jr. Hudson Institute's Center for Soviet and Central European Studies evaluates economic, social, and policial change in this region. The Center is interdisciplinary and future-oriented, seeking to contribute to formation of enlightened U.S. and Western policies toward the USSR and Central Europe. Richard W. Judy, formerly Professor of Economics at the University of Toronto, is Director of the Center.

The *East-West Forum* is an organization for research and policy analysis, sponsored and funded by the Samuel Bronfman Foundation. Based in New York and Washington D.C., its goal is to generate high-quality analyses of public policy issues and to bring the resulting conclusions to decision makers in the political sphere. The Forum was founded by Edgar M. Bronfman, Chairman and Chief Executive Officer of the Seagram Company, Ltd., who serves as the Forum's President. In July 1989, Mr. Bronfman received one of the highest awards that the Government of Hungary can bestow on a citizen of a foreign country in recognition of his philanthropic activities. Executive Director of the Forum is James M. Montgomery, former Deputy Assistant Secretary of State for Congressional Relations. The Forum's chairman is Seweryn Bialer, Blefer Professor of International Relations at Columbia University.

Indiana University is one of the major public research and teaching universities in the United States, with a faculty of more than 2,000 and an enrollment of 86,000. Its main campuses are located in Indianapolis and Bloomington. The Russian and East European Institute is one of the largest and best-known in the country, coordinating the area-focused research, teaching, and learning activities of about 50 professors and hundreds of students in the university's College of Arts and Sciences and in the professional schools. Indiana University has numerous professional links to Hungary. For example, the only endowed Chair of Hungarian Studies in the United States is located at Indiana. Its School of Business helped to establish and participates in the International Management Center (IMC) in Budapest. The School also conducts an annual seminar at the IMC for Western corporation executives, and it is developing a series of executive programs for Hungarian managers, sponsored and in part funded by the World Bank.

Nomura Research Institute is a leading private research organization in Japan which offers a wide range of services in the information field to both private and public sector clients. Headquartered in Tokyo, it has a staff of more than 2,800 persons and is global in scope, with offices in New York, Washington, D.C., London, Hong Kong, Singapore, and Sydney. The Institute conducts macro- and micro-economic surveys, investment research, and studies of government policies. It also provides advice to government organizations in the formulation of policy, consulting services, development of information systems, and systems integration. Mr. Koichi Minaguchi, who is a member of the Blue Ribbon Commission, is the current President. The Institute is one of the associate research organizations, along with BI (U.S.), IFO (Federal Republic of Germany), IFRI (France) and RIIA (U.K.), of the Tokyo Club Foundation for Global Studies, which was established in order to conduct joint international economic policy research. Mr. Minaguchi is the president of the Foundation.

István Hetényi	Paul Marer
Co-Director	Co-Director
Blue Ribbon Commission	Blue Ribbon Commission

Appendix C:
Biographies

Márton Tardos

born in 1928, experienced the national trauma of social disintegration between the two wars and Hungary's defeat in the Second World War during his formative years. He was attracted to an ideology which called for a society governed and managed by new, enlightened men. Over the course of his university studies and later working in the National Planning Office between 1953 and 1956, he prepared himself to take part in such a mission. The October 1956 Hungarian revolution radically changed his outlook and his life. He realized that the possibility of organizing society from above was very limited, and that weakening democratic and market mechanisms leads to catastrophic consequences. Since then he has worked, in his research, on how to transform the directive-planned economy into a free market economy. Since 1956, Márton Tardos has held positions at the Hungarian Chamber of Trade, Institute of Business Cycles and Market Research, the Institute of Economic Sciences of the Hungarian Academy of Sciences and the Financial Research Ltd. Beyond this, he has taught at the Budapest University of Economic Sciences and lectured at several American and European universities. He is the author of numerous publications.

Sylvia Ostry

is a native of Winnipeg. She received her Ph. D. from McGill and Cambridge and has subsequently been awarded honorary doctorates from 17 universities in Canada and abroad. She has taught at a number of Canadian universities and was a Research Officer at the University of Oxford Institute of Statistics. Sylvia Ostry joined the Canadian Federal Government in 1964. In 1972, she was appointed Chief Statistician of Canada; Deputy Minister, Consumer and Corporate Affairs Canada in 1975; and became Chairman of the Economic Council of Canada in 1978; head of the Department of Economics and Statistics of the OECD in 1980. In 1985, she was appointed Canada's Ambassador for Multilateral Trade Negotiations and the Prime Minister's Personal Representative for the Economic Summit. In 1987, she delivered the Per Jacobbsson foundation Lecture and received the Outstanding Achievement Award from the Government of Canada. She is at present Chairman of the Centre for International Studies at the University of Toronto. She is a member of the G-30, London. She has authored and co-authored over 80 publications, covering a range of empirical and policy-analytical subjects.

Iván T. Berend

born in Budapest in 1930, is currently the president of the Hungarian Academy of Sciences and a professor of Economic History at Budapest University of Economic Sciences. He is the author or co-author of several important works in his field, including *Economic Development of East-Central-Europe in the 19th and 20th Century*, *Industrialisation and the European Periphery 1780-1914*, and *History of the Hungarian Reforms 1953-1988*. His widely-recognized scholarship has earned him visiting professorships and fellowships abroad (University of California, Berkeley, 1978; Oxford University, St. Anthony's College 1972 and 1973, All Souls College, 1980; W. Wilson International Center for Scholars, 1982-83) as well as corresponding membership of the British and the Austrian Academy of Sciences.

Enikö Bollobás

is a literary historian and professor of American Studies at Jzsef Attila University in Szeged, Hungary. With a background of several years at various American universities and a commitment to human rights, minority and women's issues, in recent years she has played a decisive role in creating an awareness of family and feminist problems in the contemporary political and social climate of Hungary. She has written extensively on literary history and theory, as well as feminist issues. She is chair of the American Studies Committee of the Modern Philological Society of Hungary, leads the political discussion and action group *Hungarian Feminists*, and heads the Budapest office of the international Human Rights for Women network.

Csaba Csáki

born in Turkeve, Hungary in 1940, is a professor of economics and president of the Budapest University of Economic Sciences. He received his doctorate in 1971 from the University of Economics. From 1977 to 1982 he was a member of the agricultural research team at the International Institute for Applied Systems Analyis, and since then has headed the Center for Agricultural Policy Analysis in Budapest. He has held various consultancy positions with the Food and Agriculture Organization since 1979. In 1987 he was made corresponding member of the Hungarian Academy of Sciences. He is currently a member of several journal editorial boards, including "European Forum for Agricultural Economics" (FRG), "Acta Oeconomica" (Hungary), "Agricultural Economics" (Holland), and "Economic Review" (Hungary).

Guillermo de la Dehesa

has a long career of service, beginning in 1977, with the Spanish government and international organizations. His offices include: Director General at the Ministry of Commerce; Secretary General at the Ministry of Industry and Energy; Vice-president of the Industrial Committee at the OECD; Director of foreign asset management and international relations at the Bank of Spain; Secretary General of Commerce; Member of the 113 committee of the EEC; Secretary of Economics and Finance. Since September 1988 he has worked in the private sector in his capacities as C.E.O. of Banco Pastor, Vice-chairman of Goldman Sachs Europe Ltd., and as the director or chairman of several other, Spanish firms. He has been advisor to both the World Bank and IMF. He is a Member of the Group of 30 and governor of the Center for Economic Policy Research (CEPR).

Pierre (Pete) S. du Pont IV

55, is a partner in the law firm of Richards, Layton & Finger, P.A., in Wilmington, Delaware. A 1956 graduate of Princeton University, he later received his law degree from Harvard University in 1963. After six years in business with E. I. du Pont de Nemours & Company, Inc., he entered politics in 1968, serving in the Delaware House of Representatives (1968-1970), as a member of the U.S. House of Representatives (1971-1977), and as Governor of the State of Delaware (1977-1985). Pete du Pont was a Republican presidential candidate in 1988. He is a trustee of The Northwestern Mutual Life Insurance Company and The Whitman Corporation. Governor du Pont served as Chairman of Hudson Institute in 1985-1986 and continues on its Board.

Herbert Giersch

studied economics at the Universities of Breslau, Kiel and Münster in West Germany and at the London School of Economics. From 1955 to 1969 he was economics professor at the University of the Saarland in Saarbrücken, and from 1969 until his retirement in 1989 President of the Kiel Insitute of World Economics. He was a founding member of West Germany's Council of Economic Experts (1964-1970) and visiting professor at Yale University 1962-1963 and 1977-1978. Since 1960, he has been a member of the Academic Advisory Council to the West German Ministry of Economic Affairs. He has published books and articles in professional journals on international economics and economic growth.

Janos Hrabovsky

was born in 1923 in Budapest, where he subsequently received his first university degree in agricultural sciences. He also received advanced degrees in agricultural economics in Canada (University of Toronto) and the United States (Cornell). His formal education was complemented by extensive practical experience in farming and meat processing. He has taught at universities around the world (Guelph, Cornell, New Delhi and Vienna). He worked at FAO of the UN in policy analysis for twenty years and participated in four major studies on global agricultural futures and the impact of climate changes on agriculture at IIASA, Laxenburg. He is an Australian citizen, but makes his home in Vienna and Northern Italy.

Géza Jezenszky

born in Budapest in 1941, received his doctorate from Eötvös Loránd University after being barred entrance for 2 years because of his association with the 1956 revolution. Geza Jezenszky joined the faculty of Budapest University of Economic Sciences in 1976 and recently became dean of its newly established School of Social and Political Science. In 1980 he was made candidate member of the Hungarian Academy of Sciences. He was a visiting professor at University of California, Santa Barbara from 1984 to 1986. He is the author of numerous scholarly publications, including *The Changing Image of Hungary in Britain, 1894-1918* (published in Hungarian). A founding member of the Hungarian Democratic Forum (MDF), he has been a spokesman for the party from its outset in 1987. Since October 1989 he has been head of the MDF's foreign relations committee.

Koichi Minaguchi

was born in 1931. He graduated from the University of Tokyo with a degree in economics in 1955. He joined Nomura Securities Co., Ltd. that same year. From 1973 to 1984 he managed the Secretariat and then the Underwriting departments of Nomura. In 1984 he was named Executive Vice President of the corporation. In 1988 he was made head of Nomura Research Institute, Ltd. In addition to his activities with the institute, he currently serves as the president of the Tokyo Club Foundation for Global Studies.

István Orbán

was born in Budapest in 1939. In 1964, he received a chemical engineering degree from Budapest Technical University. Since then he has worked for Egis Pharmaceutical Company in a broad range of capacities from production engineering to R&D to management. In 1970 he received his pharmaceutical engineering degree, and in 1976 his technical doctorate. In 1982 he was named enterprise administrator, and in 1985 became C.E.O. of the company. In 1987, his achievements were recognized with the Eötvös Loránd Award, and the following year he became an honorary university instructor.

György von O'sváth

was born in Budapest in 1931. From 1951 to 1954 he was imprisoned for his activities in the Christian Youth Movement. After 1956, he emigrated to West Germany. He received his university degree in economics and law for the universities of Bonn and Cologne. In 1961, he worked at the Fritz Thyssen Foundation conducting research on economic cycles in the European Community. From 1965 to 1982 he served as an official at the Commission of the Communities, Directorate General for Foreign Relations. From 1982 to the present he has acted as the Head of Division in the Directorate General for Internal Market and Industrial Affairs. Since 1989, he has been co-chair of the EC Research and Documentation Centre in Budapest. He has authored several publications on economic relations between East and West and on European integration policy.

Sung Sang Park

received advanced degrees in economics from the American University and Nippon University. He began his career in banking in 1942. He has held a wide variety of positions at the Bank of Korea, including its governorship. In 1980, he was named president of the Small and Medium Industry Bank. He has also served as president of the Korean International Economic Institute, the Korean Scientific and Technology Information Center, the Export-Import Bank of Korea, and the Korean Institute for Industrial Economics & Technology, which he currently heads. He is the author of publications on development and international economics.

László Rózsahegyi

ten years after graduating from the Technical University of Budapest with a degree in electronics, founded ROLITRON Co. in 1981 to develop and produce special medical electronic equipment. In so doing, he has become one of Hungary's best-known private entrepreneurs. A key to his business success has been a strategy of overcoming obstacles of an unflexible economic and political environment in Hungary by setting up joint ventures inside and outside the country. Rolitron today is comprised of Canadian, West German, and Hungarian partners. He established the first privately owned dialysis station in Budapest. Recently, as the chief executive officer of HI-Care Dialyse und Medizinsysteme GmbH in Stuttgart, he has been responsible for managing the ROLITRON group's integration into the world market.

Hans Seidel

is the Director of the Institute of Advanced Studies in Vienna. Beginning after the Second World War, he worked at the Austrian Institute of Economic Research (WIFO), and in 1962 he was promoted to its director. In 1981, he was appointed State Secretary of the Austrian Ministry of Finance. Apart from managing the Institute of Advanced Studies, he is a lecturer at the University of Vienna, guest professor at the University of Linz, member of various scientific councils, chairman of the EFTA Economic Committee, and head of the Austrian delegation to the Economic Policy Committee of the OECD. He has authored several articles and books in the field of applied economics.

George Soros

is the President of the Soros Fund Management in New York and Chief Investment Advisor to Quantum Fund N.V.. He was born in Budapest in 1930 and emigrated to London in 1947 where he graduated from the London School of Economics in 1952. He moved to the United States in 1956. In 1979, he established the Open Society Fund and in 1984 the Soros Foundation. He now has foundations operating in ten Central and Eastern European countries. In addition to numerous articles, he is the author of *The Alchemy of Finance* (1987) and *Opening the Soviet System* (1990). He will receive honorary degrees from the New School For Social Research and the University of Oxford in 1990.

György Surányi

was born in Budapest in 1954. He received his doctorate in economics at the Budapest University of Economic Sciences in 1979 and was admitted to the Hungarian Academy of Sciences in 1986. He has been a lecturer at the Budapest University of Economic Sciences since 1979. From 1977 to 1986 he worked at the Institute of Financial Research. After consulting for the World Bank in Washington from 1986 to 1987, he served for two years as counselor to the Deputy Prime Minister. Since that time he has been the undersecretary of the National Planning Office. György Surányi has co-authored a book and published several studies in the field of financial and monetary policies. He is an officer of the Hungarian Economics Association and member of International Institute for Public Finance.

István Szalkai

has been adviser to the International Training Center for Bankers in Budapest since November 1989. From 1975 to 1982 he held various positions in the Ministry of Finance, the Research Institute of Ministry of Finance, and the National Bank of Hungary. In 1983, he was appointed Deputy General Manager of the National Bank of Hungary. From 1985 to 1987 he served as an economist with the International Monetary Fund. Returning to Hungary, he became the counsellor to the Deputy Prime Mininster and then Deputy President of the National Bank of Hungary. István Szalkai graduated from the Budapest University of Economic Sciences with a doctorate in economics. He is the co-author of two books and published several articles and studies in different fields of economic policy.

Alan A. Walters

is a senior fellow at the American Enterprise Institute and a Director of Putnam, Hayes & Barlett, Inc., an international economic management consulting firm. He is also a member of the economics faculty of The John Hopkins University. He has held a number of other academic positions in Great Britain and the United States, including professorships at the University of Birmingham and the London School of Economics. He is a widely published author whose thirteen books include *The Economics of Road User Charges, Money in Boom and Slump,* and *Britain's Economic Renaissance: Margaret Thatcher's Reforms, 1979-1984.* He has been an economic advisor to Prime Minister Margaret Thatcher, the World Bank, various governments, central banks, and financial institutions. He was knighted by Queen Elizabeth II in June 1983.

István Hetényi

an economist, is the Hungarian co-director of the Blue Ribbon Foundation and professor at the Budapest University of Economic Sciences. For decades he worked for the National Planning Office and became state secretary in 1973. Between 1980 and 1986 he was Hungary's Minister of Finance. István Hetényi is a member of the Committee of Economics of the Hungarian Academy of Sciences and former vice president of the Hungarian Economic Association. He has authored numerous studies and articles on economic policy and planning.

Paul Marer

an economist, is the Western co-director of the Blue Ribbon Foundation. Professor of international business at the Indiana University School of Business, he is internationally known as an authority on the economies of the East European countries and East-West business relations. Born in Hungary, he emigrated to the U.S. in 1956. His advanced degrees are from the University of Pennsylvania. After brief stints at Columbia University and the City University of New York, he joined Indiana University, where is is also professor of Uralic and Altaic Studies. Paul Marer has been a consultant to the World Bank, the IMF, and the OECD, and he has authored, edited, or coedited eight books and numerous other publications. In 1990, he was appointed by President Bush to serve on the Board of Directors of the Hungarian-American Enterprise Fund, which is responsible for managing funds appropriated by Congress to promote the private sector in Hungary.